FATHERLESS

FATHERLESS

WHAT I WISH I KNEW AS A YOUNG BOY

KEITH B. COLLINS

iUniverse

FATHERLESS
WHAT I WISH I KNEW AS A YOUNG BOY

Copyright © 2019 Keith B. Collins.

All rights reserved. No part of this book may be used or reproduced by any means, graphic, electronic, or mechanical, including photocopying, recording, taping or by any information storage retrieval system without the written permission of the author except in the case of brief quotations embodied in critical articles and reviews.

English Standard Version (ESV)
The Holy Bible, English Standard Version. ESV® Text Edition: 2016. Copyright © 2001 by Crossway Bibles, a publishing ministry of Good News Publishers.

Living Bible (TLB)
The Living Bible copyright © 1971 by Tyndale House Foundation. Used by permission of Tyndale House Publishers Inc., Carol Stream, Illinois 60188. All rights reserved.

New Living Translation (NLT)
Holy Bible, New Living Translation, copyright © 1996, 2004, 2015 by Tyndale House Foundation. Used by permission of Tyndale House Publishers, Inc., Carol Stream, Illinois 60188. All rights reserved.

New International Version (NIV)
Copyright © 1973, 1978, 1984, 2011 by Biblica

iUniverse books may be ordered through booksellers or by contacting:

iUniverse
1663 Liberty Drive
Bloomington, IN 47403
www.iuniverse.com
1-800-Authors (1-800-288-4677)

Because of the dynamic nature of the Internet, any web addresses or links contained in this book may have changed since publication and may no longer be valid. The views expressed in this work are solely those of the author and do not necessarily reflect the views of the publisher, and the publisher hereby disclaims any responsibility for them.

Any people depicted in stock imagery provided by Getty Images are models, and such images are being used for illustrative purposes only.
Certain stock imagery © Getty Images.

ISBN: 978-1-5320-6825-6 (sc)
ISBN: 978-1-5320-6861-4 (e)

Library of Congress Control Number: 2019901599

Print information available on the last page.

iUniverse rev. date: 02/08/2019

To my two sons, Jeremiah and Zephan, and to any male looking to be the best man he can be. This book is for you.

CONTENTS

Forewords ix
Message of Encouragement to All Men xix

Chapter 1   In the Womb 1
Chapter 2   I Wish I Knew I Had Nothing to Do
             with My Father Leaving 21
Chapter 3   I Wish I Knew I Had Unlimited Potential .. 27
Chapter 4   I Wish I Knew That I Am Not a Victim 41
Chapter 5   I Wish I Knew That My Faith Charts
             the Course of My Life! 53
Chapter 6   I Wish I Knew That My Self-Worth
             Is Not Linked to My Achievements 67
Chapter 7   I Wish I Knew That the Number of
             Girls I Could Sleep with Did Not Matter.... 77
Chapter 8   I Wish I Knew That Being Male
             Came with So Much Responsibility 89

Chapter 9	I Wish I Knew the Value of Mentorship	101
Chapter 10	I Wish I Knew That Reading Would Change My World	113
Chapter 11	I Wish I Knew That What I Do Today Will Affect My Tomorrow	121
Chapter 12	I Wish I Knew That Managing My Finances Was So Important	133
Chapter 13	I Wish I Knew That Taking Care of My Mental Health Mattered	145

Final Words of Encouragement 153
Bibliography 155
About the Author 157

FOREWORDS

My childhood was filled with occasions when I disobeyed my parents. I can vividly remember one time in particular. As I skipped into the local shopping mall, my father leaned down beside me and said, "Stay close to us at all times." I did my best to obey the order, but I was distracted by all the amazing toys in the storefront window displays.

I managed to stay close to my parents until a new toy that I had never seen caught my attention. I stopped to admire it for a split second, and when I turned around, my parents were gone. I frantically looked in every direction, but they were nowhere in sight. Terror filled my chest, and I screamed at the top of my lungs. I was lost in the middle of a busy mall, and I didn't know what to do.

Have you ever been lost?

We've all experienced the feeling of being guided in the wrong direction by our navigation systems, or feeling lost in a room filled with strangers. It's not a good feeling, and we try to avoid it at all costs. We crave the security of knowing where we're going and how we are going to get there.

Sadly, many men are experiencing the feeling of being lost in today's society. They lack role models and direction. However, they don't scream out in terror like a kid separated from his parents at the mall. They walk around in silent frustration, trying to figure out where they're going and how to get there. This has created a perpetual cycle of fatherlessness that's slowly destroying society.

Here are some shocking statistics that illustrate the problem:

- According to the US Department of Health, 63 percent of youth suicides are from fatherless homes, which is five times the average.
- Ninety-two percent of all homeless and runaway children are from fatherless homes.
- The Center for Disease Control says that 85 percent of children who show behavior disorders come from fatherless homes.
- Research by the Texas Department of Corrections shows that 85 percent of all youths in prison come from fatherless homes.
- The National Principals Association reports that 71 percent of all high school dropouts come from fatherless homes.

I could go on and on.

The cycle has been perpetuated by the media. Men are portrayed as fools, and their importance is frequently diminished. The American male has taken a posture of passivity, which has led to the rise of the independent woman. Father's Day has been hijacked because men aren't embracing their roles as leaders. Fatherhood and men in general are in a disappointing place.

This is not what God intended, and He does give us a hint about the solution. In Hosea 4:6, it's written, "My people are destroyed from a lack of knowledge. Because you have rejected knowledge, I also reject you as my priests; because you have ignored the law of your God, I will also ignore your children." Men are suffering because they lack knowledge, and the cycle continues.

Keith has written this book to bridge the knowledge gap. He has a passion for bringing light to the darkness that can be objectively observed in many men. This book is the navigation system needed to restore men to God's original idea. It does not contain all the answers, but it does contain the answer to one important question: What knowledge am I missing to be successful in my role as a man? It answers this question by taking you on a journey that helps you reflect on your past experiences, analyze your current circumstances, and create goals for your future. It's written with the idea that you were born with unlimited potential and it's time to maximize that potential for God's glory.

I've known Keith for years, and he is a man after my own heart because he cares about your future. We share the vision of a world where all men are maximizing their potential and using their God-given gifts and talents to make the world a better place. We share the goal of creating a new cycle for men—a cycle that results in fewer suicides, less homelessness, fewer behavior disorders, fewer youth in prison, and fewer high school dropouts.

This book is written to perpetuate more leaders and eliminate the passive posture that has plagued men for years. Keith has spent years pouring into America's youth, and he is determined to make a difference. He wants to be a part of your success story. God has given him a gift, and he wishes to serve you with it.

It's my hope and prayer that you take the time to read this amazing book and capture the unique wisdom in its pages. I urge you not to make a commitment to merely reading this book. I urge you to make a commitment to yourself. You were born with unlimited potential. It's time to maximize that potential and change the world. I believe in you, and Keith's book gives you a road map that shuts down any and all excuses.

— Carlos Hernandez,

There are certain people who, when you meet them, are memorable. It may be the way they look or how they talk. It may even be what they are wearing, but in the case of Keith Collins, it was his quiet confidence.

As a lead pastor, I meet a lot of people. Some just want to say hi or thank you, and others are in need of something. Keith was different. It was easy to tell from his posture, his facial expressions, and the way in which he spoke that he had approached me not to receive but rather to give.

In the years that followed, Keith served in our student ministry, prayer ministries, and men's ministry. He especially sought out young men to encourage them but also to challenge them. Keith has never been afraid to challenge folks to reach for the stars, to achieve their God-given potential.

His challenges are not just platitudes to make people feel better about themselves but specific steps that they can take to get there. You can see it on their faces as he talks with them, that questioning look that says, "Did he just say that to me?" But then a few months later, I talk to those same people, and I hear them say, "Like Keith always says," or "I never really believed in myself until Keith challenged me."

I didn't know where his deep passion for people, and especially men, came from until I read his book. He has been there. He knows the pitfalls and the temptations that young men without a father in the home quietly wrestle with and must work through.

It's not easy to be vulnerable, to admit what you didn't know and the mistakes you've made along the way, but he does exactly that in this book. He hasn't written in a style to receive sympathy, although you will certainly feel sympathetic about the challenges he has faced.

Keith writes in the same way in which I have seen him live his life. He is vulnerable yet unyielding in his challenge to be the man that God has created him to be. He gives real answers and specific steps to take in order to gain a new perspective. Walking in his shoes through the complexities of life, we gain new insight into the renewing of our minds and the success that is available to us all. Many of us may have grown up in or are growing up today in a home without a father. Keith reminds us we are not fatherless. We have a heavenly Father who wants to provide everything we need as men to live with joy, purpose, and passion.

This is more than a self-help book; this is Keith's story, his life. As someone who has had the unique opportunity to be a part of it, I can say firsthand that he has come out on the other side as a successful and godly husband, father, pastor, and businessman, and he is just getting started.

In a culture that has often forgotten or misunderstood the importance of the role called father comes a book by Keith that speaks from the heart and experience.

—Troy Gramling, pastor, Potential Church

Inspiration. Perseverance. Compassion. Reckless courage. Loving your neighbor. These are but a few of the virtues that come to mind when I think of my friend Keith. This man has left an indelible mark on my life and on those of plenty of others who've had the pleasure of experiencing his genuine love for people. This man has led, not bossed or ordered, around a ministry that comes into contact with hundreds of students a week. He personifies the qualities of tireless enthusiasm and energy. I've seen him crack some of the hardest-looking kids who many would walk away from. He's planted seeds of faith and love into the lives of so many who've lacked those very foundational building blocks. Impact! This narrative on learning to become a man in a fatherless culture could not have been scripted by a more caring and credible person. He leads with biblical principles. He loves with the heart of Jesus. He instills confidence. He provokes thought. The direction of my life has been permanently and positively impacted because of the friend God blessed me with. My family's life, by extension, has been influenced as well. The lessons he's taught me about being a godly man have led to many more lives being touched.

—Marvin Moran

The first time I met Keith was in ninth-grade English; he was a clueless transfer from North Atlanta High School. Our first interaction was him wanting to pay me for homework (a crime for which I'm sure the statute of limitations has passed).

After matriculating through high school and college, we've been able to share some amazing moments together, being in each other's weddings as well as sharing some amazing victories in ministry. Over the years, I've seen a man who's developed amazing character and conviction for what is right, and he is an inspiration and absolute encouragement.

Today, very few men are willing to be vulnerable, but that's what you have in this book. This book is full of vulnerability and emotion that shows how powerful the presence of a strong male role model is.

I'm truly excited about the journey ahead, and I believe that this book will truly bless you. Keith's love for God, thirst for knowledge, and pursuit of truth is evident throughout, and I believe that men everywhere could benefit from simply recognizing that we have a responsibility. As fathers, we have a responsibility to build up our children. As sons, we have a responsibility to embrace growth. As men, we have a responsibility to impact the world and lead the way.

Take the time to really soak in the words on these pages and go on the journey with Keith as he brings you into his life and takes you on a walk in his shoes.

—Jaz Vick, outreach pastor, the Path Church (Atlanta)

In a world where so many teenagers are embarking on their journeys toward becoming young adults, this book shares revelation that can be instrumental in their growth process. How I wish that while growing up I had access to a positive male mentor like this. Some of the topics such as purpose, self-worth, and low self-esteem mentioned in this book I deeply struggled with as a teenager becoming a young adult; looking over my life, the phrase "I wish I knew" echoes through my mind. As mentioned in this book, there are many decisions we have all made that would have been different had we known better, and this book is a testament to that. The author goes deeply into his personal journey of becoming a man while experiencing some of the struggles we have all faced. The insight into his journey can be healing for others who are facing similar struggles. The chapters in this book are easy to read and straight to the point. I have no doubt this book will play a critical role in the lives of those who are blessed to receive the revelation written in it.

—Sheldon Peterson, Next Step Training, journey coach, author, speaker

Keith Collins has written an amazing self-disclosure book about his life as an African-American boy in public housing to a college graduate and a married father of two sons. He shatters many myths about being a real man, and Keith shares his wisdom about being a responsible adult. Mr. Collins openly discusses his seeming failures and his spiritual struggles to follow God's guidance and plans for him. Keith's purpose in writing this inspirational book is to stimulate all young men to persevere to be the best that they can be! Many specific helpful tools are included in his writing: mentors, relationships, listening, reading, finding your faith, decision-making, managing your money, feedback, delayed gratification, and living in emotional balance. Reading of this powerful book is recommended to all.

—James H. Burton, Ph.D.
Author, Human Nature Meditations – Concentrations for Managers and Other Human Beings

MESSAGE OF ENCOURAGEMENT TO ALL MEN

Good sir, how are you doing? I want to take the time to let you know that though I might not know you, I believe in you. I don't know who has ever told you that in your life, but I really do believe in you. That's the reason you have this book in your hand. It's because I believe it is my life mission to encourage men and boys all over the world to push past any limitation that has come into their lives. There are many limitations that hinder us from moving and achieving our greatness; it could be a father walking out of your life, a bad breakup, not understanding your true potential, or just not believing that you're worth it. I want to let you know that you are! You are worth it. You can change your life. Where you are today is not where your tomorrow will be. Your best days are ahead of you.

You might wonder how I can be so confident in what I'm telling you. I believe that there is a Creator who created you.

And that Creator created you in His image, which means you are not an accident. As my pastor Troy Gramling would say, "You did not wash up on a shore, you did not fall from a tree ... you were created on purpose for a purpose." That's the core of my belief, and I'm willing to go through the awkwardness of this conversation with you to communicate that truth to you. I'm going to say it: I love you. So does the Creator. I believe in God- the Creator. Now if you don't believe in God I understand there are many life experiences that could hinder someone from believing in God; and that's okay.

God has inspired me to write this book, specifically for you. It is something that has been on my heart for the last couple of years, and it has pained me—and I have been burdened with helping men take full responsibility for improving themselves and being the best they can be. So I have started on the journey to reach, empower, and encourage men like yourself.

You might wonder how in the world I can help you. Well, I know you have probably experienced hurt in some way or another, and I want to let you know I have too. You might have experienced pain. I want to let you know that I have too. Those experiences might have been caused by another person, such as them leaving; you weren't the one who made a bad choice. These experiences allow us to relate to each other.

Sometimes our past haunt us. I want to let you know that you are more than your past. The decision you made in your past is exactly that—your past. It holds no weight in your situation today. If you have taken that experience and made a valid attempt to learn from it, you are on your way to better days. You are not your past, so don't hold on to it. In the words of Eckhart Tolle, "Sometimes letting things go is an act of far greater power than defending or hanging on." I believe this world needs the best version of you, and you can't give this world that if you are holding on to your past. You might say, "I don't care what this world wants from me." That's absolutely fine. But I do believe that it is not right to live on this Earth without making any contribution. If we don't contribute to this world we are part of, we are stealing. We are, as Myles Munroe put it, "generational theft." You have something inside of you that the world needs. It does not matter your race, it does not matter your creed, and it does not matter your age; you have something to offer. It does not even matter how your past looked. You have something!

Over the course of this book, you're going to learn things I wish I knew growing up and found out only as I got older—or let me say I actually listened as I got older. My hope is that you go after it. My hope is that you don't stay where you are—that you strive to reach your fullest potential. That means leaving nothing behind on this Earth, that you create every song, write every book, experience every joy, live every moment. My friend, I love you, and I want the absolute best for you. Take these words in these pages and apply them to your life. I promise you they will help you, and if you need anything, let me know, as I am your friend, your brother, your co-laborer.

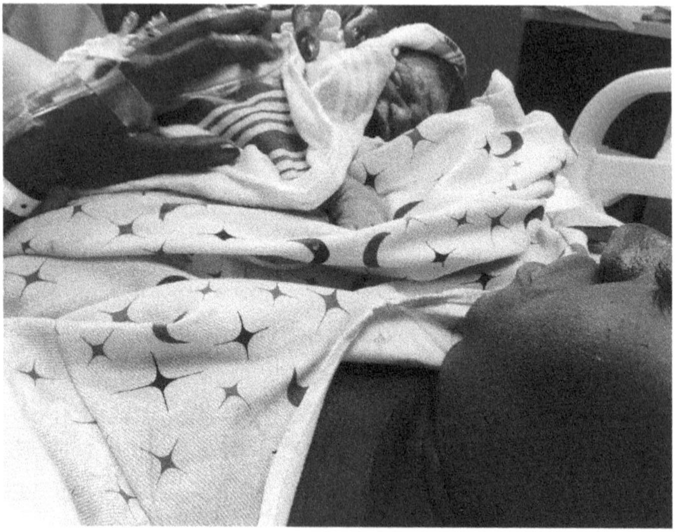

CHAPTER 1

In the Womb

Becoming a parent is the moment when all of life's battles suddenly seem worth fighting for.
—WishesMessages.com

"Congratulations, you have a little boy!" The gift and the curse. Wait a minute—I said a gift and a curse! There is no mistaking that every child is a gift. On the other hand, I believe men have been given a special, divine gift. Boys have the unique role of bringing up a society or tearing it down.

I am a man with many life experiences that I believe can help you, whether you are 12 or 112. I have learned a lot from my life, and one thing I know is when you learn from experience, it creates a wealth of knowledge for you to share with others. My hope is not to change you but to inspire you to do and become more. In order to do that, I will draw from my life experiences.

My Story

I was born in Atlanta, Georgia, in Bankhead Courts Zone One area, in the 1980s. I was raised in a single-family home a good majority of my childhood—from the ages of three to eleven, to be exact. My mom and dad split up when I was three years old, and I can still remember that day. See, my mom and dad got into an argument, and there was a knife involved. I remember my dad's arm bleeding and him grabbing me by the shoulders and telling me that he loved me. I did not know that was the last time my mom and dad were going to be together as a couple. Over the next couple of years, a string of males came into my life, but none would fully commit to being the father figure I desperately needed at the time. My dad and I had one of those see-you-on-the-weekend type of relationships. Don't get me wrong; my dad made every attempt to make sure that on the weekends, the spent time together was fun and meaningful. We would do things like go fishing, play basketball, and go to church.

My mom second husband entered my life when I was around eleven, and that was the first time I had that everyday father figure in my life. They are still married, and he is still a great and vital role model in my life.

Living in Atlanta, I commuted to middle school. Then I went to two different high schools. The first one was where, for the first time, I got a taste of multicultural living. What that means is I went to school with black, white, and Hispanic people from all different nationalities. It was a great opportunity for me to learn how to deal with people that came from different backgrounds outside of my own. Up to that point, I had only experienced hanging out with my kind, black people. The high school I went to was in a small town called Douglasville, Georgia. My high school was called Lithia Springs High School, and I learned a lot about transportation. That was when I got my first car, and being a high school student, that meant the world. While in high school, I had my share of normal high school experiences—from dating, to sports, and finding out how I measured up socially with other people.

College was fun and a great time of developing myself into the young man I am today.

When I first started college, I was going for computer science. Like most other students, I looked at a list of jobs, found out who made the most money, and then decided that was the career path I was going to take. Let me tell you something: calculus is hard! While I was in college, I took Calculus I and found out I would have to take Calculus II, along with a host of other math courses that seemed too difficult for me, so I changed my major. At the time, I had been working for Six Flags Over Georgia for about two years, and I thought that business and management was fun and that I could make a good living doing it. So I switched my major to management and marketing. It was around this time that I met an amazing young lady by the name of Stania.

Stania and I met through Facebook, which was uncommon at the time. Back in 2007, it was kind of weird to meet someone on the internet, and if you did meet someone, it was because you had no game. Our relationship grew throughout our college years. We both were ambitious for the things we wanted in life. It was in college that she and I grew our relationships with God, and it led to a pretty cool conversation in year two of us dating. One day, Stania came to me and told me that she heard from God while reading God's word, and He told her that she and I were going to get married, and our first child was going to be a boy, and we were to name him Jeremiah. You can only imagine how this freaked me out as a guy, to hear all of this coming from a girl I was dating, when I really didn't know at the time if she was the one for me.

As we continued to date over the next two years, we found ourselves growing closer and closer. Stania graduated a year before I did, with a degree in accounting. If she was going to move back in with her parents, it mean moving back to Florida from Georgia. She found herself with no place to go and no job after college in Georgia, so our relationship was at a crossroad. This crossroad forced us to make some really tough decisions, but make those decisions together with future goals. I remember the day we sat down at a Seattle's Best Coffee in Douglasville, Georgia, and put a list together of dreams and goals for the next couple of years of our lives. On that list was for me to move to Florida, get married, find a job, get a place for us to stay, and start a family. Then we prayed to God and asked Him to help our plans to succeed, which is one of the things He asked us in Proverbs 16:3 (New International Version), "Commit to the Lord whatever you do, and he will establish your plans." Then we prayed as if it depended on God, and we worked as if it depended on us. Side note: any step of faith always requires action.

Over the next year, some pretty amazing things happened for Stania and me. Stania found a local church in South Florida where she volunteered, and it eventually led to her getting a job there. We were able to get engaged on my spring break of my senior year of college, and during that time, I had a couple of job interviews and then secured a job. Things were moving so quickly that on May 7, 2011, I graduated with my degree in marketing and management, on May 12, 2011, I moved to Florida, and on May 17, 2011, I started working with a company I had previously worked for.

Stania and I are parents to two amazing young men, Jeremiah and Zephan. We have bought and sold a house, have eliminated the word "debt" from our vocabulary by paying off $32,000 worth of consumer debt, and are moving toward all the things that God has planned for us. I have been in youth ministry over the last five years and have had the opportunity to speak and impact the next generation of middle school and high school students. I am grateful for every day that I have been able to impact others.

So what gives me the right or credibility to write this book? I'm a young man in my thirties, a father of two, and a husband for six years, and I have been with the same lady for the past eleven years. I grew up watching my father and mother split up. I've seen things that boys should not see. I have experienced things that I believe can help any man in any area of their life. One of my life goals is to be able to inspire and create better men, to inspire them to be better fathers, which will ultimately change the world. I believe that everything rises and falls on the leadership of the male in the household, whether positive or negative.

This book shall be the catalyst to help all men, all over the world, be the men they are called to be. My hope and prayer is that you take my life experiences and learn from them to set you up to be better than I ever could be. I am not saying that I am perfect, but I am striving to reach my fullest God-given potential to be the best husband, father, leader, brother, and son that I can be.

Now let us take a look and explore how we can become better men! I'm excited to go on this journey with you. Let's begin.

The Role of the Male

According to Dr. Phil in a 2005 article, "If men want to be successful in their marriages and family life, they have to change and broaden their definition of what it means to be a successful as a man!" (http://www.drphil.com/advice/the-role-of-the-man-in-the-family/). Pause: that's such a bold statement. Dr. Phil goes on to say that being a good provider, protector, leader, and teacher is a privilege that comes with responsibilities that many men are not aware of. There has been a misconception of what it means to be a real man. Think about when you turn on the TV or look at social media and you see a real man; he is tall, strong, bold, and never emotionally affected by anything that goes on around him. Many of us have been fed this lie, and it has cost us dearly. There are men and women who have been brought up to believe that men are supposed to be tough and macho and never show emotions. To help dispel some of the rumors attached to men, we must look at two perspectives regarding the role of the man in the home. The first is a social perspective, and the second is the biblical perspective.

Social Look

Let's look at what society has told us about being a real man. To help us with that, I want to look at the article that Dr. Phil wrote.

Most men believe that to be a man, you must be a provider and protector. Although there is some truth to that, we have received a blurred view of the two words. In this context, the word *provider* is associated only with a man providing financially for his family. For most men, the mere act of going to work and collecting a paycheck to provide food, clothing, and shelter for the family fulfils the role of provider. To be honest, it's something a woman could do it too.

What if, as a man, the money you make does not fully cover the food, clothing, and shelter needs for your family? Can you say you are a true provider for your family? Please know when I ask these questions, I am not trying to poke fun at you if you have encountered some type of struggle or hardship that has made it difficult to provide for your family financially. My goal is to challenge your thinking in this matter.

Do you remember, as a kid, having playground arguments with your friend about whose dad could beat up whose? I surely do! We all saw our dads as protectors, but is that the true definition of a protector? I encourage us to look at the word "protector" as a person or thing that prevents harm from happening to someone—seen or unseen. Here is why my definition is a little bit more spot-on when it comes to the role of a man as a protector in the household: to defend and protect your family from physical harm is good, but what about the unseen and emotional harm? How do you protect your family members' self-esteem and self-worth? If we are to consider ourselves protectors, we must protect on all fronts and enlist any help needed to do that.

Now that we have covered "provider" and "protector," let's take a look at two more perspectives we should consider when defining a successful man. According to Dr. Phil, men are to be considered leaders and teachers in the home. Now, when I say leaders and teachers, I am not talking about in the same context as a leader of a company or a teacher in the classroom. So often, as men, we put all our efforts into things outside of the home, forgetting the invaluable opportunities we have at home.

When I talk about leading the household, I am talking about having a following. John Maxwell says that leadership in its simplest form is influence. People with influence have a following, and people with a following take people places. To take people places, you have to have a goal. Sometimes, as men, we don't have a direction or a goal for our families, where we see ourselves in the future. Too often, we miss the opportunity to influence our families due to the lack of vision for our families. Now don't get me wrong; you can be present and have no influence on your family. The best scenario is to be physically and mentally present with a clear vision for where you want your family to be in the future, as a man. When we have a clear vision of where we as men want to see our families, we will also teach in our homes as we deal with life situations.

Men are to be the teachers in the home. When I say teachers, that's not to say that women can't teach; this book is meant to highlight the impact of men in the household. When we as men teach in the home, we take the different situations that life presents us and leverage them to help our families go to the next level. We also teach our families by the examples that we set in our everyday lives.

Biblical Look

There are two dominant views when it comes to the role of men: societal and biblical. The social views of a man's role is heavily external. Within this section, we will look at the biblical role of a man. Before we start down the path of me quoting scriptures, I want to quickly state that I believe the Bible is a collection of books that is designed to help you and me best function with others, and the Creator Himself gave it to us. Now, you might not believe in the Bible, and that's okay, but I do know if you were to just read it and apply some of its teachings, your world could radically change for the better. Now let's look at what the Bible has to say about manhood.

Lead

Men were created to lead and steward the land and relationships God gave them. In Genesis 1:26–28 (English Standard Version [ESV]), it says, "Then God said, 'Let us make man in our image, after our likeness. And let them have dominion over the fish of the sea and over the birds of the heavens and over the livestock and over all the earth and over every creeping thing that creeps on the earth.'" As you can see, early on, man was given leadership responsibility. For the sake of this book, we will look at the man's leadership responsibility in the home in the context of marriage. In the list that follows, there are some verses that speak to the responsibility of men in the marriage relationship.

Responsibilities of a Man

- "Likewise, husbands, live with your wives in an understanding way, showing honor to the woman as the weaker vessel, since they are heirs with you of the grace of life, so that your prayers may not be hindered" (1 Peter 3:7 ESV).

- "But if anyone does not provide for his relatives, and especially for members of his household, he has denied the faith and is worse than an unbeliever" (1 Timothy 5:8 ESV).

- "For the husband is the head of the wife even as Christ is the head of the church, his body, and is himself its Savior" (Ephesians 5:23 ESV).

- "But I want you to understand that the head of every man is Christ, the head of a wife is her husband, and the head of Christ is God" (1 Corinthians 11:3 ESV).

Love

As men, we are called to love. Now you might say to yourself, "I am not the mushy type." That's fine. I'm talking about the love that is a choice that is based off of a biblical truth. Love is a choice; it is a conscious decision, not something you fall into. Often, in movies, you see people fall in love. Love is not just an emotion or a feeling; love is much more than that. Love is a commitment. Love is the foundation of any and all great relationships a man might find himself in, whether it's in a marriage, friendships, or the role of father. Love is the ability to care for someone and back it up with action. In a couple of places in the Bible, it mentions great insight when it comes to the word love. Here are a few:

Love in the Bible

- "Husbands, love your wives, and do not be harsh with them" (Colossians 3:19 ESV).

- "Love is patient and kind; love does not envy or boast; it is not arrogant or rude. It does not insist on its own way; it is not irritable or resentful; it does not rejoice at wrongdoing, but rejoices with the truth. Love bears all things, believes all things, hopes all things, endures all things" (1 Corinthians 13:4–7 ESV).

- "Beloved, let us love one another, for love is from God, and whoever loves has been born of God and knows God. Anyone who does not love does not know God, because God is love. In this the love of God was made manifest among us, that God sent his only Son into the world, so that we might live through him. In this is love, not that we have loved God but that he loved us and sent his Son to be the propitiation for our sins" (1 John 4:7–10 ESV).

Instill Faith

A lot of things that we as humans do are modeled after what we see others do. Think about a little baby learning how to talk for the first time. We spend hours talking to a baby, hoping they'll pick up some of the words we have communicated to them over the months. As fathers, it is our responsibility as the spiritual head of the household to instill godly principles into the family through our actions and leadership. A father modeling faith sets up a solid foundation for a family to be blessed for generations. Just to make it clear, I am not saying that a woman has no role in the modeling of faith to her family; I am just saying the primary role/responsibility was given to the man. Here are some verses that speaks to the male's role to instill faith:

Fathers Instilling Faith

- "Teach a child to choose the right path, and when he is older, he will remain upon it" (Proverbs 22:6 The Living Bible).

- "And if it is evil in your eyes to serve the Lord, choose this day whom you will serve, whether the gods your fathers served in the region beyond the River, or the gods of the Amorites in whose land you dwell. But as for me and my house, we will serve the Lord" (Joshua 24:15 ESV).

- "Fathers, do not provoke your children to anger by the way you treat them. Rather, bring them up with the discipline and instruction that comes from the Lord" (Ephesians 6:4 New Living Translation).

His Positive Impacts on Society

It is a beautiful thing to see man operating at the fullest capacity because it impacts society in a positive way. One of the biggest positive impacts men make is in the area of fatherhood. Through fatherhood, a lot of life situations can be modeled out in homes for the kids, such as how to deal with conflict, showing love to your spouse, and how to have a relationship with God. Positive fathers can teach a young boy how to become a man. It's through the father that a young boy can learn what is true in the mix of all the chaos and noise that he hears in the world. It's by teaching his son that a father is able to leave a legacy.

A positive father figure in the house helps a young lady to know her value and worth. When a young lady has a father who loves her and shows that love to her on a daily basis, when she is approached by a young man who does not have the right motives, she is easily and quickly able to see the young man for the fraud that he is. The father protects the young lady from certain heartbreaks because of his influence on her and love for her.

When a positive father is active in the schools, there are fewer behavior problems. I remember one time when I was in about fourth grade, I decided to give my teacher some trouble. My mom was tired of spanking me herself, so she called my father. Keep in mind that at this time, my mom and dad occasionally argued over the phone about different things I needed for school, money, and his being present in my life. I thought there was no way my dad would come to the school to discipline me for my behavior in class, but boy was I wrong. I'll never forget the day he came to the school and pulled me out of class to the bathroom. Let's just say he never had to show up at school ever again. As I grew up, there were other times my dad had to step in and discipline me for my behavior or grades. It helped me and shaped me to become the man I am today. Throughout high school, I was able to take care of my schoolwork because I understood that I had what it took, and I had a father who was concerned with what I did. That's not to say my mother did not have a hand in it as well; trust me, she did.

Fathers have the ability to alter how dating is done. A father has the ability to teach his son standards that are the bedrock for a solid relationship, simple things like holding the door for a woman, paying for the date, and making sure boundaries are set up before the courtship even starts. These are things a father must teach his son to set his son up to win daily. Now, this might contradict everything you hear and see in mainstream media today, but the father is the one who is to lead the family in this area.

A father's role is also to model what hard work looks like. Hard work is not commonly taught in today's society. We live in a culture that is fixated on instant success. The father can give his kids chores that will help instill many different life skills that will help the child succeed, not only in school but also in the workplace. Without this solid foundation, a child can be on a path to laziness—with many different consequences. Overall, a solid work ethic should be taught in the household and modeled by the father.

Effects of Not Having a Father in the House

When there is no father in the household, it causes chaos, and society as a whole suffers. Think about it—prisons are filled with men who never had a father figure. Many of these men seek the approval of other men through the avenues of gang, crime, and other cries for help.

When I was in college, my world was rocked by one book, *Wild at Heart* by John Eldredge. In this book, it talks about three things that guys search for: number one, a battle to fight; number two, a beauty to rescue; and number three, an adventure to live. Through that book, I learned that when there is no father in the home during the monumental moments of a boy's life, a void is created. When you have a monumental moment in your life—whether it's hitting the game-winning shot, scoring a winning touchdown, or making the grade you want—and you look around to seek the approval of your father, and he is not there, it creates a void. Those voids create questions that build up inside a young man's heart: *What's wrong with me? Why didn't he show up? How can I earn his approval?* I'm not going down this whole self-pity road. I am simply communicating how a child's life can be drastically changed because of a father. There were times when I just wished that my mom and dad would get back together so I could have a normal family. I realize now that there's no such thing as a normal family.

When there is no father figure in the house, boys cannot see hard work modeled. Though it can be modeled by a mom, there is something about the dad showing the son simple things related to work—putting forth your maximum effort, taking pride in what you do, and doing work that is constructive to society as a whole. Often, I come across young men who want all the things associated with hard work but never really want to do the hard work. You see it portrayed on TV—the overnight success. There is no such thing as overnight success. The only true success is one that takes years of practice and hard work. When I think about fathers who take pride in what they do, I think about my pop. He was not my biological father, but he was the father figure that impacted me the most. He owns his own painting business, and man, he worked hard. I remember hours and hours of watching him work when I was younger. He would leave the house early and come home late. When he finished his work, he had so much pride in it, and he would often take me to the job site to show off what he had done. He often took before-and-after pictures of projects to show how far they came. I credit a lot of my work ethic and the ability to just go after it to him. Because of his example, I have been able to outwork a lot of other millennial I've come across.

The dating scene can be affected in a negative way when fathers do not properly train their young men. The father's role is to guide and mold a son to be a gentleman, teaching him to treat a lady with respect, keeping personal standards for himself. It impacts others in many different ways. I think about how important it is for a young man to be able to value a lady and see her as a queen or a helpmate rather than a piece of meat or an object to satisfy a physical desire. The sole responsibility of training up the young man and daughter is not just placed on the father; it is placed on the mother as well, and society battles against anything that a positive, faith-centered household is going toward. There are movies and TV shows that objectify women and glorify men who were able to have multiple sexual partners and not make the lasting commitment of marriage. When the dating scene is not done right, the man doesn't even think about marriage. This saddens me to my core and is one of the reasons I've put this book together.

Overall, I believe it is of the utmost importance to mold men while they are young so they can be the foundational pieces in society that we need them to be. But it starts in the home, and it starts today.

Why Is It Important to Mold Them While They're Young?

"Train up a child in the way he should go; even when he is old he will not depart from it"
(Proverbs 22:6 ESV).

"Children are a heritage from the Lord, offspring a reward from him. Like arrows in the hands of a warrior are children born in one's youth. Blessed is the man whose

quiver is full of them. They will not be put to shame when they contend with their opponents in court"
(Psalm 127:3–5 New International Version [NIV]).

To me, it is very simple why we train children. It is biblical, and you will leave a legacy that exceeds your own life. In the Bible, it talks about training up children in the way they should go, so when they get older, they will not depart. This is so good because it teaches us as men to set a foundation to help children have a pathway to follow. This training does not mean to browbeat them into submission; it means to allow them to grow and explore and figure out what their natural gifts and abilities are. By doing this, you set the child up for future success. To train a child up requires being present in the child's life and observing the gifts and talents that the kid naturally possesses and then investing in those skills and talents. As a parent, when you set your child up to succeed by investing in their future, ultimately you invest in your future and your legacy. There'll be nothing that says we lived if we don't pour ourselves into our children. In the movie *Black Panther*, T'Challa had a time to speak with his dad, and his dad told him if a father has not prepared his son for his death, then he has failed. Those words cut me like a knife, because I'm a father of two boys, and my life goal is to set my kids up for future success so they can be all that God has created them to be. If I do that, and I'm an awesome husband, I feel that I have succeeded in this life. But how many fathers do we know who have not given it a second thought? God speaks about kids being like arrows that are shot out into the world—so they are little Keiths running around that have some of the core DNA that I have. The question is, Do I want little ticking time bombs who are unable to make life decisions, or those who possess boldness and stand up in the face of oppression? Or those who stand up for what they believe in? Or those who take the right action in difficult situations? Do I want kids who will just go with the flow and live a life that, when you look at them on their deathbed, leaves you saying they never lived at all? Ultimately, it's the child's choice, but it's our choice as fathers, and our role as men, to lead and guide our children. It is our role and responsibility to equip them with the many skills and talents we have learned. If we are able to do these things, we will be setting them up to win. We are sending out arrows out into this world, and we can have impacts that supersede our lives. This is the life I want to live, the life I have been given, and the life that is important to me. All of this starts when a child comes out of the womb.

Review

1. What do you believe is the role of a male, in your own words? Why?
2. How did you know you were a man?
3. What lies have you been told as a boy about manhood?
4. What legacy would you like to leave for your family?
5. Do you believe you have the power that is described in this chapter? Why or why not?

Halloween 1991 3 & 4 year old class
Keith & Rionne

CHAPTER 2

I Wish I Knew I Had Nothing to Do with My Father Leaving

> A child should never have to assume
> responsibility for a parent's decision.
> —Keith Collins

Have you ever heard this story? The guy and girl start dating, they love each other, and next thing you know, they have a kid. Unfortunately, life gets a little bit hard, and there are disagreements in the house. There is no real commitment to the relationship from the man to the woman, and the only thing the two share is a child. For whatever reason, the guy decides to leave, so the mother and child are left to fend for themselves. This is a story that has plagued so many of the children in our society. More than 35 percent of the kids in America are living in homes without a father (https://www.npr.org/sections/ed/2017/06/18/533062607/poverty-dropouts-pregnancy-suicide-what-the-numbers-say-about-fatherless-kids).

Who is to blame for the absence of fathers? We could point the finger all day, but I do know who is not to blame. If you are reading this book right now, you probably have been affected by not having a father figure in the house or having a strong bond with your father. I want to let you know that the actions of your father are not your fault. When you say the word *father*, you are assuming that the person having the kid is an adult, and adults are responsible for their attitudes and actions. With that being said, no child can cause a father to walk out on them. The choice is up to the father, whether it's because of insecurity about being able to provide or not getting along with the mother. Those are just some of the reasons why a father might leave the house. I wish I had known that it was not my fault that my father left.

When I was in middle school, I remember having to visit my dad's house on the weekend and hanging out with him and his family. I remember comparing my living situation to theirs and thinking that they had it better. I would sometimes ask myself, *What was it about me that caused my mom and dad to split up?* I started to believe I had some part to play in my dad leaving. Often, I felt undervalued. It was through no fault of my dad; it was the internal dialogue that was going on in my mind. Now, I'm not saying your father is a saint. I know no one is perfect. But I do know that my father, for the most part, was trying to do the best he could with what he had. I just did not see it at the time. When I got to high school, the low value I felt intensified as I became more active in sports.

In high school, I was able to play a variety of sports. I often had my stepfather there to support me in the crowd and cheer me on. It felt great to have someone in my corner giving me the *yeah, that's right, you're doing it* feeling. But there was a small piece of me that longed to see my father there, to see the man who helped create me support me in the crowd. I think we yearn for the approval of our fathers; we want to be able to please them because it helps us feel valued and confident.

Upon entering college, I started to put my finger on the feeling I had when it came to my connection with my father and the void I felt. I took full responsibility for the way I was feeling, and I scheduled a time to talk with my dad about how I was feeling and the effect that their splitting up had on me, up until this day. I shared with my dad how at times I felt empty and undervalued, and I shared with him how I longed to see him and my mom back together many times. Finally, I shared with him that I forgave him and held no ill will toward him. That one phone call started to change the trajectory of our relationship.

Now at the rightful age of thirty, my dad and I have a close relationship. I call him in times of need. We often call each other two to four times a month just to catch up, and to be honest with you, I would drive up from Florida to Georgia right now to get a hug from him. There's something about the security factor in a hug from my dad that can never be replaced. That is something I share and cherish with my sons.

It's Not Your Fault

Your father may have made a decision that took him out of your home when you were growing up as a child. This might leave you with a feeling that you had something to do with it. I want you to know that it is not your fault. Often, we develop a negative outlook on a situation like this because there is an enemy that wants to hinder our growth. In the Bible, it is described as the devil, and he looks for ways to destroy (John 10:10). When we take the blame off ourselves, it allows us to move with a new sense of freedom. My friend, I want you to know that regardless of your path, the actions of your father are not your fault.

You Can Only Control Your Attitude and Actions

I want you to remember this: you can only control your attitude and actions. I cannot make you read another page in this book. I cannot make you happy right now. You are the only person who can do those two things. So, regarding the male figure in your life and his effect on you, you have the power to allow it to hinder you from the greatness that lies inside of you, or you can use it to help you be better in your relationships. You can use it to impact others.

Turn Your Mess into Your Message

One thing I will challenge you to do is take the mess that has happened in your life and make it your message.

In the next couple of chapters, you will discover how to do just that by looking at my life story.

Review

1. What has been your experience with your father in your life, and how has it affected you?
2. Do you blame yourself for your father's decisions?
3. Have you had an open conversation about any hurt that you might have felt coming up? If so, how did it turn out?
4. How can you apply what you have learned in this chapter?
5. How does your upbringing and relationship with your father change how you father your kids?

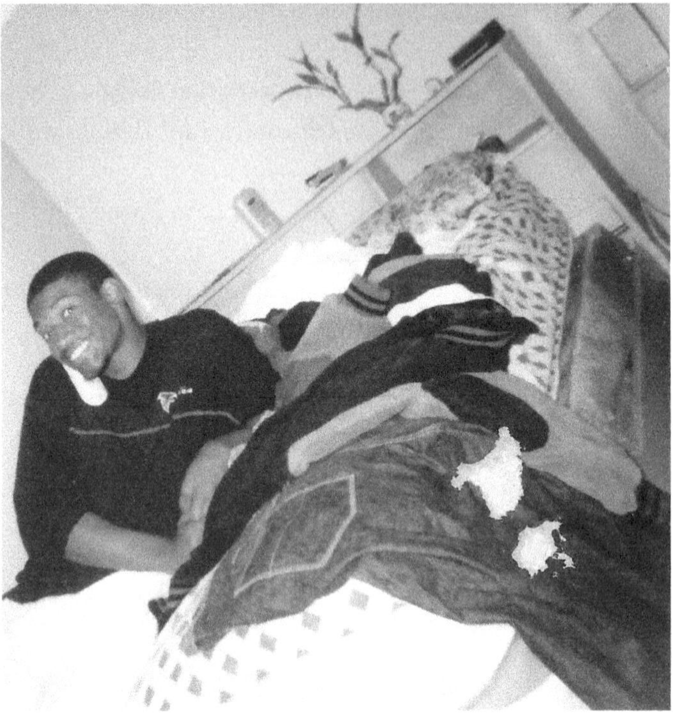

CHAPTER 3

I Wish I Knew I Had Unlimited Potential

The only person you are destined to become
is the person you decide to be.
—Ralph Waldo Emerson

Cut from the Basketball Team

When I was in eighth grade, I was lucky enough to play football. It was awesome for me. To give you some insight on my physical makeup as a middle school student, I was five eight, 170 pounds of pure muscle and a little bit of fat. I was the star center for our team. Yeah, I know it's a glamorous role and a position that most middle school aged students cannot handle well. Let me tell you about my middle school: we had pride. We had been undefeated for the past six years prior to me playing. So you can imagine the pressure I was under. Because of the events at the World Trade Center on September 11, 2001, our first football game was canceled. That following week, we had our first official football game of the season, and we dominated. The first play of the game was a touchdown run by a guy named Alex C., a mammoth of a middle school student. He was six two, 210 pounds, and solid muscle. He ran so hard the first play he ran out of his shoe. He also had a Barry White type of deep voice, one that sounded like Val Venus from WWE, "Hello Ladies."

That year, we were able to keep up the streak; we went 5–0 for the season. I was able to start every single game. The season was filled with highs, lows, and new opportunities to grow. Toward the end of the season, and often during practice, one of the coaches would talk about basketball and how the season was quickly approaching us. For me, that was another opportunity to be a star; at least that was what I thought. One of the coaches told me, "Keith, if you want to try out for the basketball team, I'll make sure I cut you." I took this as a little challenge from the coach. I really gave it my best so I could make the team. Boy, was I wrong. I tried out for the team and gave it my all but did not make the team. I went to the coach and told him that there had to be some type of mistake because I was one of the best players I'd ever seen. He told me that he knew I was going to get mad and that I just didn't make the cut. Now I knew there were some very good players on our team, and there were some guys already dunking in middle school, but I thought

I had a chance to make the team. After the coach made the cuts, he told us that if we still wanted to try out, a spot might open up. I did it for a week or so, but another guy and I still did not make it. One of the guys who did not make the team stuck it out and just worked on getting better. Eventually, he made the team! Now that I look back on that moment in my life, I see that he knew the importance of having unlimited potential. He knew that who he is today is not going to be the same person he is tomorrow. That was a lesson I would have to figure out some other time. Middle school passed, and then it was time to enter high school.

Wrestling for Two Years

In high school, I played a number of sports. I was able to play football for two years, baseball for one year, and wrestle for two years. One of the sports I enjoyed the most, believe it or not, was wrestling. I avoided playing the sport for the first two years of high school because I did not want to be one of those guys grabbing other guys in a tight spandex outfit. The thought was culturally unintuitive. My first year taking part in the sport was my eleventh-grade year, and I did okay. I don't remember my record, but I'm quite sure it was more losses than wins. I had fun during the season, though, and I was able to grow and develop myself along with the different techniques needed to win matches. My senior year, I did even better. I came one win away from going to state. Wrestling, to me, is one of those manly sports. It's you and the opponent, mano a mano, no-holds-barred, and there is nothing to get in between you and your opponent.

Wrestling was a sport that pushed me many times to my breaking point—whether it was the long miles of running, the intense practices, or the discipline to eat the right things so I didn't gain weight. Wrestling had a special place in my heart, and toward the end of my senior year, I regretted that I wasn't willing to tap into the sport earlier in high school because I missed out on some of the potential I had to become very good at the sport. I sum up my experience with wrestling with this quote: "you don't know what you don't know until you know what you don't know." I didn't know how much fun I would have or how much I would grow as a person until I joined the sport. Unfortunately, I missed out on two years of high school wrestling because I had been unwilling to step out of my comfort zone.

Comfort zones have a way of keeping us locked in and not exploring different opportunities that the world has to offer. So when I got to college, it was time to explore. When I went to college, my mind-set was to get the piece of paper so I could go out and make a real difference by having a job. But it was in college that I met some amazing teachers who were able to challenge my thinking and impact me in such a way that I became more of myself. I remember taking business management courses, sales courses, and marketing courses; all were designed to help me bring out my true self. In fact, two teachers influenced me the most and helped me to realize that I had something special about me.

My Confidence Grows in College

The first teacher was Dr. Eric Bergiel. He taught my management classes and was a joy to be in school with. It was in his class that I developed a lot of my understanding for what management is and what it is not. It was in his classes that I discovered how important it was to ask questions as a student. Also, I developed the confidence in my ability to study, and know what materials were needed for the tests. My love for learning and my confidence in my abilities as a student grew while I was in this course. Those were invaluable lessons that I took to other classes.

Dr. Burton had an unorthodox style of teaching. At the end of every class, we would hold hands and sing songs, which was weird for me and a lot of the other students in his class. We learned invaluable life skills that weren't taught in high school and would not be taught in any other environment outside his classroom. He valued us as students, and in his class, I was able to learn about my ability to go after my full potential. In fact, he told me how I would change the world. Inside of his classroom was one of the first times I heard it said that I, Keith Collins, had the ability to change the whole trajectories of the seven billion people who populated the world. I often look back and think about this teacher and how he impacted me, and I can't help but be so grateful for having crossed paths with him. After I finished his classes, he normally nominated one student to help teach his classes over the next semester. I was fortunate enough to be that student! I would take part in the teaching his class twice a week for a full semester, and after each class, we would go have lunch together and just talk about life. Needless to say, a connection formed between us that continues to this day. We do share one experience that most students and teachers don't share. We were invited as a class to join him for his seventieth birthday. He was going to do something usually not done by someone at the age of seventy. He was going to jump out of an airplane. That's right; you heard me—jump out of an airplane. He was going skydiving, and he invited everyone in his classes to come along. Only one other student and I took him up on the offer, and that one experience showed me how I was starting to become a man who stepped outside of the crowd. I was starting to reach my full potential.

Now at Thirty

Upon graduation, I knew there was more for me, and I wanted to go after it. In 1 Corinthians 2:9 (New Living Translation), it says, "No eye has seen, no ear has heard, neither has it into the hearts of men what God has in store for those who love Him." I graduated from college, and it was now time to take on the world, and I knew just how I was going to do it—or at least I thought so. After graduating, I moved to South Florida and started working, in hopes of making tons of money. As I started to work and chase the American dream, I quickly saw what was really important to me—receiving all that God has for me and being the best version of myself that I can possibly be. When I left my hometown in Georgia, I knew that at some point I was going to be involved in ministry, but I never knew when that would be.

Growing up, there were two things I never wanted to be a: a police officer and a pastor. I've heard it said that God has a sense of humor. After working for a year and a half at the company I had previously worked for, I started to take note of the people I was surrounding myself with and where

I wanted to be in the long term. I noticed how my future self and my current self were not part of things that would allow me to achieve what I really wanted. As I mentioned earlier, I had dreams of making a real impact in people's lives while having an amazing marriage and a family as well. Upon entering adulthood, I started to read a lot of books, and one of the things that struck me most in the books I was reading were two things: Number one, you can tell where a person is going to be in the next five years by the people they associate with. Number two, don't take advice from anyone who is not where you want to be in life. Those two things helped me decide to make a career change and step into full-time ministry.

Ministry was nothing like I expected. My first thoughts were that we would stand around the church and pray all day. The minister gave me an opportunity to discover and understand that God had so much more in store for me. I think of the parable of talents that goes like this: A man goes on a journey, but before he leaves to go on his journey, he leaves three of his servants a certain amount of talents (money). To the first servant, he gives one talent. To the second servant, he gives three talents. And to the third servant, he gives five talents. When the man comes back from his long journey, he goes and talks to the servants to see what they did with the talents he gave them. He goes to the third servant and asks him what he was able to do with the talents he was given. The servant replies, "I took the talents you gave me and created five more." When the master heard this, he was thrilled and said, "Because you were faithful with what you were given, I'll give you even more," and so the third servant received five more talents in addition to the talents he already had been given. Then the master went to the servant that had three talents and asked, "What did you do with the talents you were given?" The servant replied, "I took the three talents that you gave me, and I was able to go out and create two more talents." The master replied, "That is awesome. Because you were faithful with what you had, I'm going to give you more." And he blessed him with two more talents. Then the master came to the first servant and asked him what he did with the talents he was given. The servant replied, "I knew you were a harsh and cruel master, and I was afraid to lose the talents you gave me, so I hid them and I buried them." The master looked at him and said, "You wicked and selfish servant. You could have done something to invest those talents to make more, but because you did not even try, I will take your talents back." And the master took his talents and gave them to the other two servants. And I do believe that story sums up my workings in the church.

I took the talents that I knew of, naturally talking to people and connecting, and I multiplied the talents to learn how to do many other things, and God used me and blessed me in so many ways. I have been able to speak on stage in front of thousands of kids. I've been able to impact the lives of families. I have been able to motivate and inspire kids to go after their dreams. I have been able to take leaps of faith for God and watch Him do incredible things because of my obedience. One of the things I've been able to do, along with my wife, is test God in the area of our finances. In 2013, my wife and I were expecting God to do big things in our lives, and our church normally does an annual giving campaign. This was the year that we decided to step out and be bold to see what else was inside of us in terms of the spirit of our generosity. My wife and I committed to giving way above and beyond our normal tithes in hopes of starting a family and owning a home. We knew God had much more in store for us, and we wanted to test the waters to see how much he had in store for us. So that year, we gave like we had never given before, and we watched God open major doors. We wrote on the stage during that time, and one of the things we wrote was that we were going to have a child, and we wrote Jeremiah's name on the stage. That year, Jeremiah was born. We also wrote that we wanted a house, and that year opened the door for us to own our first home. That story in itself was really crazy. I signed an offer letter for the house before I ever saw the house with my own eyes. I took a total step of faith—one I am proud of.

In this season of life, I'm excited for all that God has placed in front of me and how it has grown over these last couple of years. There are countless stories about how I discovered the potential I have inside of me, but this would make the book a little too long. Just know that God has given you unlimited potential, and it's up to you to reach out and go after it.

The Definition of Potential

Google describes *potential* as having or showing the capacity to become or develop into something in the future. Another definition is the latent qualities or abilities that may be developed and lead to future success or usefulness. I describe potential as the ability to be better tomorrow than you are today. That means every day, every moment, we have the opportunity to step into our potential. The you that you are now is not good enough to be the you of tomorrow, so there is a constant improvement that you and I always need to be working on. Some of the skills, talents, and gifts already live inside of us. You might say to yourself, "Man, my potential has been crushed … I have no potential." That is a lie. Each and every one of us has potential, because we have the opportunity to grow.

Examples of Used and Unused Potential

I see "used potential" as the person who is striving to do, be, and have more for themselves without harming others. I believe potential can be reached in categories—such as reaching your health potential, reaching your spiritual potential, and reaching your financial potential.

"Misused potential" is when you put your critters in the wrong areas. When you do nothing at all to improve your overall quality of life. When you take your skill sets and use them to harm, mislead, and manipulate others. These are examples of misusing your potential. We're all called to be stewards of the potential we have in us, and it is up to us to use them in ways that will overall increase the quality of life for ourselves and others.

How Do You Know You Have Unlimited Potential?

You are not a dog or a cat. Now, you might think, *Of course I know that.* The main difference between us and animals is the fact that we can grow and change. When you look at a dog or cat, no matter what happens, no matter how much time goes by, the animal stays true to its nature. If you were to see a dog today and come back and visit it in the next five years, it would still be doing the same thing that dogs normally do. That is not so for you and me. We are human beings. We get a chance to evolve and change our lives on a daily basis, based on the thoughts we think, the life experiences we have, and our desire to think and see ourselves as being more. We are not stagnant creatures; we are constantly evolving. That's one of the main things that helps me to know, and gives me the ability to tell you, that you have unlimited potential.

I'm a huge advocate for what the Bible says about me! And God's Word has something to say about my potential. In John 14:12–14, Jesus is speaking to his disciples and us today, and this is what he has to say. "Truly, truly I tell you, whoever believes in me will do the works I have been doing, and they will do even greater things than these, because I am going to the Father. And I will do what ever you ask in my name, so that the Father will be glorified in the Son. You may ask me for anything in my name, and I will do it." I am a living, walking, and breathing testament to this very thing. Over the past couple of years, I have been asking God to show me how I can impact others outside of what I am currently doing. He gave me the idea of creating and writing this book. This is one example of me stepping out and reaching after my full potential. I am hoping and praying that this simple example serves as an encouragement to you, to let you know that you have more inside of you. So, go after it.

With that said, I know some of us might be a little skeptical, still trying to figure out how we reach our potential.

How to Reach Your Potential

Know what you want, discover the price it takes to get it, and go after it.

A lot of times, we don't get what we want out of life or certain situations because we don't know what we want. We have many options and choices to do and become anything. But we simply don't decide. There is so much power in making a decision or figuring out what you want, so much so that words cannot describe it. The only thing I'm asking of you is to sit down and have some quiet time with yourself and your Creator. Ask Him to lay upon your heart what He wants for you, or tell Him what is in your heart. Everything starts with knowing what you want.

After you know what you want, you must take a look at what price needs to be paid in order to reach your goal. This is important because sometimes the thing we want has a price associated with it that we are not willing to pay. At the time of writing this book, there is a new iPhone out, and although I want a new phone, I'm not willing to pay the price associated with this new phone. It's the same for our dreams. Depending on our seasons of life, there might be dreams that are best achieved during different stages. I'm not saying you should not go after them; I'm saying figure out a way and a time to go after them that will be most effective to achieve the results you are looking for.

And finally, I'm going to say this again and again and again. Go after it. Go after it. Go after it. Go after it. Go after it. Go after it. Go after it. At the end of our lives, we will be faced with tons of thoughts. I do not want those thoughts to be, *I wish I did more.* Allow God to work in your life so you can reach your fullest potential through Him.

Review

1. When was a time that you discovered you had potential?
2. Have you ever had someone see more in you than you saw in yourself? If so, how did that affect you?
3. What is a dream/goal that has been placed in your heart?
4. How can going after your dream/goal positively affect society?
5. What obstacles do you need to break through to achieve this dream or goal?

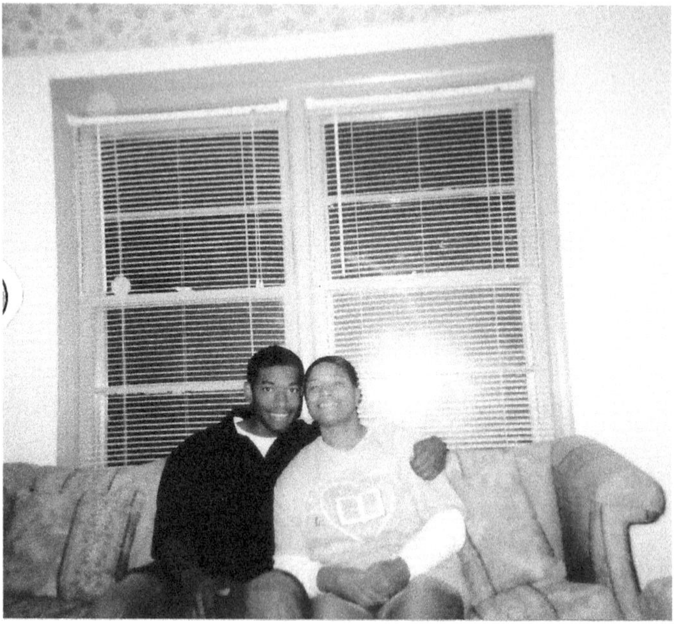

CHAPTER 4

I Wish I Knew That I Am Not a Victim

No one can make you feel inferior without your consent.
—Eleanor Roosevelt

In My Neighborhood

I lived a good distance away from my middle school, so I had to take public transportation. My mom had the great idea that she wanted me to be better than her, so when it came to choosing a middle school, she chose one that was different from where everyone else in the neighborhood went. To this day, I am thankful for that, but at the time, I did not understand why she would have me catch a bus to a school in a different location. Because I went to another school, I would have friends in the neighborhood picked on me. They would say things like, "Your mom is afraid to let you go to our school because you would get beat up." I would give the rebuttal, "My mom wants me to be better than her. That's why she's having me to go to different schools." Eventually as I grew up, the middle school that the neighborhood kids went to got turned into an alternative school for kids who misbehaved, and my middle school is still a thriving middle school in the community.

During my middle school experience, I recall having moments where I felt like a victim. This was before I knew what the word victim meant. One of the moments was in our neighborhood while playing basketball. We would split the court up into two sections—one side with young kids, one side for the older kids, and occasionally the other kids would try to play the whole court while we were having a game on the younger kids' side. In this situation, the other kids rarely asked if they could run a full-court game, as if our game on our side was not important. I can remember countless times in the middle of scoring the game-winning shot, when we were getting close to the end of a game, and then next thing we knew, the big kids were playing and running down our end of the court. It was one of those moments when I felt like there was nothing I could do. It was also one of those moments when you I felt like, *Hey, did you not notice that I'm here?* In that situation, it was hard not to feel like a victim. Also, as a kid growing up in the projects in Atlanta, the environment was something I could not change. I'm talking about the Section 8 apartments, where everyone knew there were people who did drugs, and the rent was well under a hundred dollars, based on your economic situation.

I had to work with what I was given. I remember having to encounter dangerous situations in my environment. One time, my mother and I were walking home from catching public transportation, and someone who was walking with us was shot in a drive-by. He was a mere twenty feet behind us when he was shot. That was the same path that we had to travel every day when I got off the bus. I still remember the bloodstain that was left on the concrete for days. I also remember the color and the type of vehicle that was involved in the drive-by and having to see that vehicle in the neighborhood on a daily basis, wondering if that person was going to start shooting again right as I was passing the car. These are some of my middle school experiences that led me to feel more like a victim.

I Could Not Change Things

In high school, I remember wanting to change my life circumstances. One of the main circumstances I wanted to change was the fact that I did not have my biological father in my life. My mother married her amazing second husband, who has been the father figure in my life since then. There was still a part of me that longed for my family to get back together. This was more so when I was in ninth grade and I would see families together. Growing up in my neighborhood, I didn't see a lot of family moments. When I got to high school, my parents moved into a house. I would go out to Walmart or different stores, and I would see families together. I would see the mom, the dad, and the children laughing, having a good time. I longed to see my biological father and my mom together, all of us happy. I felt like I was a victim of my circumstances.

What I failed to realize at the time that with the addition of my stepfather, I was able to have a father figure in the house. To have someone leading us gave me many different life opportunities. I also gained a little sister, who lives with me. So truthfully, I had the family that I was looking for and wanted. I just had to realize that I had it. I was caught up in this ideal version of my life, which caused me to feel more like a victim, because it was not exactly what I wanted and because it wasn't perfect. I didn't value it as much as I should have. I don't know where you are in your life, but you might be having a moment where you are not valuing something that is right in front of you. You might be in a situation where it seems like there is no way out, that all hope is gone, that God cannot help save you. I want you to know that being a victim is a choice. You can choose how you want to live out the rest of your life.

I was able to expand my way of thinking and understand that I can control more than I thought. I believe my thought process changed when I read the statement, "You can control two things in this world—the first one is your attitude, and the second one is your actions." I think I read it in a John Maxwell book, *Attitude 101*, and that statement revolutionized my life. At the time, I was working at a theme park in Georgia. I was in a leadership role and often had to deal with kids who did not want to work. I had to learn how to motivate them and myself to do a task, and at the time, it seemed meaningless. Helping in the season and teaching that you control your attitude and your actions gave the people I led a sense of power. Truthfully, it gave me a sense of power, just being able to control who I am within any given time. I love to use the analogy of "no one likes to be a puppet." If other people can control how you move, act, live, and breathe in a certain situation, then they are your puppet master. They pull your strings, and you respond. That's no way to live; being tossed back and forth like a rag doll just means that you are unstable. And during college, I was able to learn how to be more stable and not be a victim of the circumstances that were around me. In James 1:8, it says, "A double-minded man is unstable in all his ways."

I wanted to be a stable person, so I started to grow in this area, and it led to dramatic change in my life.

I Know Everything Happens for Me

I learned to walk with a sense of confidence because I know that everything happens for me. You might ask yourself, "Keith, how in the world does everything happen for you?" This is a mind-set I have chosen to pick up and to live inside of my life. When I say, "Things happen to me," it relinquishes any control I have for changing my situation. When I say, "Everything happens for me," there's an opportunity for me to grow and to have some sort of control in the situation, which relieves me of having to feel as if I am a victim in a given situation. Another cool perspective that I have today is that no matter what happens in my life, God is able to help me. I'm a strong and firm believer in the verse found in Romans 8:28 (NLT), "For we know that God works all things together for the good of those who love Him and are called according to His purpose." This verse was written by Paul, and he endured so many different situations that could easily have given him the feeling of being a victim shipwrecked, left for dead. Instead, he persevered to write the verse we just read. That's the kind of life I want to live, that's the kind of life that changes lives, and that's the kind of life that honors God. Ultimately, you and I get to decide if we want to be victorious or have a victim mentality.

What Is the Victim Mentality?

The victim mentality is an acquired personality trait in which a person tends to recognize themselves as a victim of the negative actions of others, and they behave as if this were the case. It's similar to the Eeyore syndrome, where everything is happening to you and it's all doom and gloom. This does not have to be the case. And by the end of this chapter, it is my goal to help you move out of that state. So here are some questions to ask yourself.

How do you know if you have a victim mentality?

Does everything happen to you? As I mentioned earlier, when things happen to you, it relinquishes any ability to change your circumstances. You find yourself saying, "Things like this always happen to me." Or, "That's just my luck." These are words of effect.

Do you feel that everyone is out to get you? In the victim's mind, everyone has banded together to take over your life and make you miserable. It can be the waitress who forgot to get your order correctly at the local restaurant, or it can be the parent who told you some invaluable information you did not want to hear. It could be the judge who just follows through on what the law says, and you find yourself serving time.

Do you put yourself down? Do you ever say to yourself, "I never get things right"? Do you not see the personal value you bring to the world? Do you not give yourself credit for your accomplishments, no matter how big or small they are? Free advice is available all day; you can always encourage yourself by telling yourself something positive.

Do you enjoy telling people about tragedies that happened to you? This question is designed to help you see if you enjoy others' sympathy. Sometimes we do this without even knowing. We tell sad stories and share awkward moments to get people to say how much they care and feel for us and feel sorry for us. We tell people who will see it the way we see it, to gain more support for why someone has wronged us or about situations not in our favor.

Do you relive past pains or hurts often? Do you relive the argument over and over again in your head, the one when you and that other person got into a confrontation? Does it give you a sense of peace to be able to get mad at them again? This is not the behavior of a winner. You were called to do and be more. Let go of that past hurt.

How to Conquer a Victim Mentality

I bet you're like, "Man, I do not want to stay a victim for the rest of my life. How can I change this victim mentality?" I'm glad you asked. Here are a few action steps that you can take today to start seeing change in your life.

Admit the part that you played in any situation. This is taking personal responsibility, and it allows you to be able to control you. Situations happen that we can't control, but what we can control is our attitude and reaction. It is important to gain a mind-set that will allow you to feel empowered as a man, whatever situation comes your way. You have the ability to change your perspective in all situations.

Forgive yourself. Often, we do not forgive ourselves because we feel we need to be punished more than we have been in life. This keeps us thinking how bad of a person we are. Forgiving yourself is not saying that you have done nothing wrong; it is you choosing not to beat yourself up over the next ten years for something you did in the past. We all make mistakes. It's not about the mistakes we made; it's about how we rebound from those mistakes.

Seek new perspectives when facing new situations. Seeking counsel from people outside of yourself gives you a different perspective. It sometimes give you a clear head about a small issue that seemed like a big one. Having those people around you with structured thinking allows you to move closer to your purpose in life.

Create a grateful journal. Often, we end up with a victim mentality because we are no longer grateful for the little things in our lives. By keeping a grateful journal, you recall positive moments in your life. This allows you to be thankful and grateful. By being grateful, you focus your eyes on the positive things, as opposed to the negative things, and this keeps you away from the victim mentality. Just to give you a hint, I'm grateful you have taken the time to pick up this book and start the process of changing your life.

Serve others. Serving others is a great way to get our eyes off ourselves and onto others. While serving, you gain a different perspective that allows you to grow as a person. In fact, some of the people who serve find themselves being the happiest they have ever been in their lives. Serving others balances the scale of life. When we serve others, we share the spotlight on other people's situation and our ability to help them.

You are victorious. You are more than a conqueror. Allow these words from Paul to soak into your heart.

> What, then, shall we say in response to these things? If God is for us, who can be against us? He who did not spare his own Son, but gave His all for us—how will He not also, along with Him, graciously give us all things? Who will bring any charge against those whom God has chosen? It is God who justifies. Who then is the one who condemns? No one. Christ Jesus who died—more than that, who was raised to life—is at the right hand of God and is also interceding for us. Who shall separate us from the love of Christ? Shall trouble or hardship or persecution or famine or nakedness or danger or sword? As it is written: "For your sake we face death all day long; we are considered as sheep to be slaughtered." No, in all these things we are more than conquerors through him who loved us. For I am convinced that

neither death nor life, neither angels nor demons, neither the present nor the future, nor any powers, neither height nor depth, nor anything else in all creation, will be able to separate us from the love of God that is in Christ Jesus our Lord. (Romans 8:31–39 NLT)

Review

1. Where does your perspective on life come from?
2. When have you ever considered yourself a victim?
3. Do you consider yourself one now? Why?
4. What do you need to deal with that you have not yet dealt with?
5. How can Romans 8:31–39 improve your perspective on life?

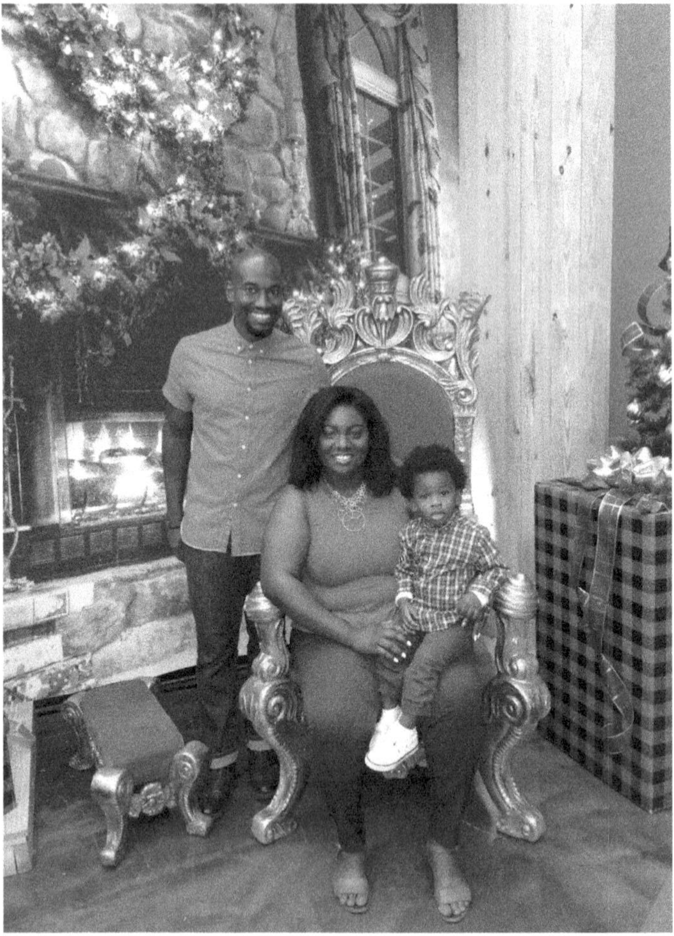

CHAPTER 5

I Wish I Knew That My Faith Charts the Course of My Life!

Faith is the art of holding on to things your reason
has once accepted in spite of your changing moods.
—C. S. Lewis

Always Thinking I Was in Trouble with God

The goal in this chapter is to let you know how faith played a major role in my life. Don't get me wrong; if you're not a religious person or anything like that, that's absolutely fine. My goal is to show you how it has played a role in my life. I do understand we all have different backgrounds and different life experiences that have made us the people who we are today. You might have been raised in a church environment, where family members were hypocrites who said one thing and did another. You might have been raised in an environment where all you did was go to church, and when you got older, you said you would not go. That choice is completely up to you now. You might be a person who cannot see how anyone can believe in something that they cannot physically see, and therefore you have dismissed religion and God altogether. That's your choice as well. Dale Carnegie said, "A man convinced against his will is of the same opinion still." My goal in this chapter is not to convince you of anything, only to display facts based upon my life, in hope that they will give you a better understanding of why I wish I knew faith at a younger age, so you can grab hold of its possibility.

When I was raised by split-up parents, sometimes I went with my dad to worship with him, and I went with my mom to worship with her. My dad was a Jehovah's Witness, and being raised in that environment as a middle school student was somewhat different. For me, that religion was more legalistic. I was not able to celebrate Christmas, birthday parties, and a whole host of man-made holidays. As a kid, I couldn't understand why it was so important to follow the religion, but I was able to grasp the importance and the need for having the Bible—God's Word—in my life. I remember many times sitting down at the table with my dad, and he would read the Bible with me and my brother and my other siblings, and I remember learning and gaining insight on how to become a better person. When I would attend their services, I had to dress up in a suit and sit through many teachings that were long and a little boring, being woken up every time I fell asleep. It felt like it wasn't relevant to what was going on in my world. I also started to believe that the end of the world would happen every single year. I did not understand it completely, but I always thought that I had to be doing the right thing to gain God's approval.

On the other side, my mom went to the traditional Baptist Church. Need I say more? The pastor would yell and scream and tell people that they would be going to hell if they didn't change their ways. It made me think I had to always be performing amazing works to gain a relationship with God. I thought He was a never-satisfied, always-judging man sitting up high, looking down at all the people like ants. As I grew up, my perspective started to change as I spent more time learning who God really was. Don't get me wrong; middle schoolers can know they need a relationship with Him, but I still thought that the relationship meant just doing awesome deeds and not sinning.

Thinking I Could Put God in a Box

During my high school years, my family and I moved, and that meant we found a different church. My dad was still Jehovah's Witness, but my mom and our family went to a nondenominational church. This church talked a little bit more about God's grace and forgiveness and His wanting for us to have a right relationship with Him. I thought I could have a relationship with Him, the kind I could put in a box for certain areas of my life.

I understood to trust in God with my everyday life and my salvation. But I did not think He could be placed in the box in terms of my relationships with girls. That led to me experiencing and pursuing girls in my high school years that could have ultimately saved me a huge headache. I thought that if I compartmentalized God's role in my life, everything would be okay. But let's think about that. God is the creator of the entire universe—at least I believe so—and I want to put a cap on His ability to change my life. How is that even possible? If I'm able to put Him in the box, and He ceases to be God with the power that I say He has, He doesn't really exist. So my understanding of God in my high school years was completely wrong because I was trying to put him in time-out, when he created the time-out. But my understanding of God would improve as I went to college.

During college, I started to realize that I needed a personal relationship with God. When I think about most relationships, whenever there is conflict, there is an opportunity for intimacy to develop. That is usually the case for people who are committed to watching their relationship grow and be the best it can be over time. So, my relationship with God grew when I was in college, largely because I found myself being vulnerable. While I was in college, I saw God more than I did up until that point in my life. I would go to Bible studies on my own, go to church right before work, and spend time reading His Word with my girlfriend at the time, Stania. This is not to say I was a perfect human being during this season of my life, but I was striving to become a better person and understand God's role in my life. I remember times when I would cry because of the level of difficulty of my work assignments, and praying and asking God for help.

FATHERLESS

The next day, a teacher would reschedule a test, or I would receive the answers to a problem from out of nowhere.

During this season of my life, I had no problem telling people that I followed Christ. In one of my classes, where I would always pray before tests, I invited the whole classroom to join me, and many times, the other students would join in as well. There came a time when I did not tell everyone that I was praying, and then they would say, "Keith, are you going pray or what?" And then I would pray. I remember that class being filled with a sense of joy. I remember us getting good grades as well. I'm not saying if you pray before your test without studying and doing those things, you're going to get an A. What I am saying is that the relationship with God that you develop allows you to be bold and confident with others who are around you in a positive way.

Toward the end of my college career, I found myself in a situation where I needed more faith than ever before. Let me give you the scenario. I was a senior, and my girlfriend had just recently moved to Florida. We had previously talked about making our relationship become more serious, and me moving to Florida was one of those ways. I did not know where I was going to work once I graduated, but I did know that it had to be in Florida. I remember doing interviews with companies in Georgia and asking them if they had anything available in Florida, explaining that if they didn't, it would not be a good fit for us. One time I was talking to the HR vice president of a multibillion-dollar company, and I told him that I was not able to do anything with this company because they were not in South Florida. Talk about faith! I remember going to the company that I was currently working for at the time, at the beginning of that year in 2011, and telling them that by May 2011 I would no longer be there, that I would be in South Florida. They said, "Oh great! Do you have a job there?" I said no. They asked, "Where are you going to live?" And I said, "I don't know, but I know I'm supposed to be there."

This level of boldness I had was not just because of luck. On New Year's Eve of that year, I went to the church I was a part of to pray and bring in the new year. I remember the speaker saying that to achieve all that God has for you requires faith. I remember reciting the verses before the teacher even spoke, and that night was a monumental night because that was the night I decided I was going to move to Florida, and I truly knew it was going to happen. That led me down the path of seeking wise counsel to see if it was the right move. I remember going over to one of my church member's houses and asking for leadership and guidance. He told me something that I had literally asked God for before I entered the house, and that was confirmation that I was on the right track.

I Grew My Relationship with Jesus

Now that I am thirty, I've come to the strong understanding that I personally am in charge of my relationship with God. I can decide how much of Him I want or how little of Him I want. All of this is in accordance with my faith. What I mean by that is my willingness to put myself in situations where I have to show that I trust and believe God. Faith is like a muscle that you develop over time, just like going to the gym. You can have seasons where your muscles are huge, and you can have seasons, like my currently one, where you are a little bit flabby. But I understand and know that there is nothing that can happen to me on this earth that I cannot persevere through, because of my relationship with God. This relationship has been the bedrock or cornerstone of everything I say and do—and one of the main reasons I'm writing this book. Faith is so important to the growth of a Christ follower. In fact, without faith, it is impossible to please God (Hebrews 11:6 NIV). By now, you might you ask yourself, "What is this whole faith thing?" Well, I'm glad you asked.

What Is Faith?

Faith is defined in many different ways on the internet. It is described as having complete trust or confidence in something or someone. Another definition of faith is a strong belief in God or in a doctrine or a religion based on spiritual apprehension rather than proof. I somewhat disagree with the second definition, the point of it being based on spiritual apprehension rather than proof. I have tons of proof for my faith. The things I have talked about are my trust and belief in Jesus Christ. Now you might not believe any of the Bible or even that God exists. I'm absolutely fine with that. I ask that you track with me over the next few moments, not to change your mind but for you to just explore with me as I explain my faith.

Gospel of Jesus Christ

As a follower of Christ, I believe in the Gospel of Jesus Christ. The Gospel is described in this way: God Created man in His image (Genesis 1:27 NIV), to have a relationship with Him. Humankind no longer was perfect when they ate from the tree of the knowledge of good and evil (Genesis 2:17 NIV). This is called separation between God and man; because God is perfect, He can't associate Himself with sin. Sin is a picture word for missing the mark. It's like you are target practice and you are trying to hit the bull's-eye and you can't hit it, that's what sin is. God loved man so much that He was willing to send his only begotten son to die for our sins (John 3:16 NIV). God raised his son up from the dead on the third day, and because of the belief in what God did, I can admit that I have done wrong and receive the gift of everlasting life (Romans 10:9–10 NIV).

I am aware that my faith hinges on the fact that Jesus Christ rose from the grave. I am convinced that He did, but you if are not, I challenge you to do three things. One, ask God to reveal Himself to you. Second, do your own research. I have two book recommendations, *Mere Christianity* by C. S. Lewis and *The Case for Christ* by Lee Strobel. Third, take action on your findings.

Why Does Faith Matter?

By now, you probably have asked yourself, "Why does this matter?" Faith matters because it has the ability to help us in many different areas of life. My faith has relinquished self-doubt, insecurities, and fear about everything that is going on around me in school, home, work environments, and my marriage. Your life can be better than what it is, and I am convinced that Jesus loves you enough not to leave you where you are.

Why Faith Matters

I Discovered My True Identity in Christ

The cool thing about having a relationship with Jesus Christ is that you gain insight into who you truly are. You learn that you are created in God's image. Then you can consider yourself to be His masterpiece, which changes everything.

The freedom that I experience in Christ comes from understanding that the weight I tried to put upon myself… I don't have to carry it and was not designed to carry it. Sin required there be a death, and Jesus Christ dying on the cross meant that punishment was no longer my burden to carry. That also gives me freedom because I understand that when things happen today—whether planned or unplanned—God is working everything out for my good.

Relationships

My faith in Jesus Christ taught me to have better relationships with others because that is one of the foundational principles within my relationship—to be that of a servant, to think of others as better than myself and love others as much as I love myself. These are traits that allow me to make a difference in my life and others' lives.

Peace

My faith has given me so much peace. There's a sense of confidence that I have when I face certain situations that allows me to be unshakable. My faith in God has grown to allow me to understand that the things that happen to me are temporary and never permanent. Now I am convinced that God is able to work all things together for my good, and that gives me peace. In the Bible, it describes this peace as a peace that surpasses all understanding.

Hope

We live in a world where people have no hope. A majority of their hope is in the government or people who are majorly flawed. My hope is in God, the author and the finisher of my faith. My hope is in the one who created me and has a specific purpose for me in this life.

Body of Believers

Since I gained a relationship with Christ, I've been able to surround myself with a body of believers. It is a group of people who believe what I believe, which has given me strength to face a lot of situations. I found that when I associate with people who believe the same foundational beliefs that I do, I am able to draw strength from them in times of need. Don't get me wrong. I can learn from anyone in a situation. One other positive thing about being a Christ follower is that you have other believers who believe what you believe and who have experienced similar things you have, which can give you wisdom and confidence.

The One Catch with Christianity

You have free will, which means you are not a robot. You are technically free to do whatever you want, whenever you want, but that does not mean you should. Having an awesome relationship with Christ requires work. No one else can grow my relationship with God but me, and I am held accountable for what I do. My relationship with Him is important.

How to Get Some Yourself

You might be saying, "Keith, how can I gain some of the peace you have?" It is very simple: gain a simple relationship with Jesus Christ. I will explain how to do so.

The ABCs of Salvation

Admit

Confess to God that you are a sinner, that you miss the mark from time to time. Repent and turn away from your sin. "Repent" means to change your way of thinking about a situation. Romans 3:23 (NIV) says we all have sinned and fall short of the glory of God. By admitting we have done wrong in the sight of God, we are being honest with ourselves that we are not perfect, but He is.

Believe

Trust in Jesus as God's son and believe that God sent Jesus to save people from their sins. Romans 5:8 (NIV) says, "In this way while we were still sinners, Christ died for us." Belief is not a mental assent; it's a confidence that you sit down on the chair you sit down on at the dinner table.

Commit

Give your life to Jesus. Ask Him to be your Lord and Savior. Romans 10:10 (NIV) has this to say: "And if you confess with your mouth that Jesus is Lord and believe in your heart that God raised Him from the dead, you will be saved. For it is with your heart that you believe and are justified and it is with your mouth that you confess and are saved." This is where we just get honest with ourselves, no matter how difficult it is. Your future depends on it.

Review

1. How has faith played a part in your life?
2. Why do you believe what you believe?
3. How has your faith grown lately?
4. What was a key takeaway for you in this chapter?
5. How can you apply what you learned in this chapter to your life?

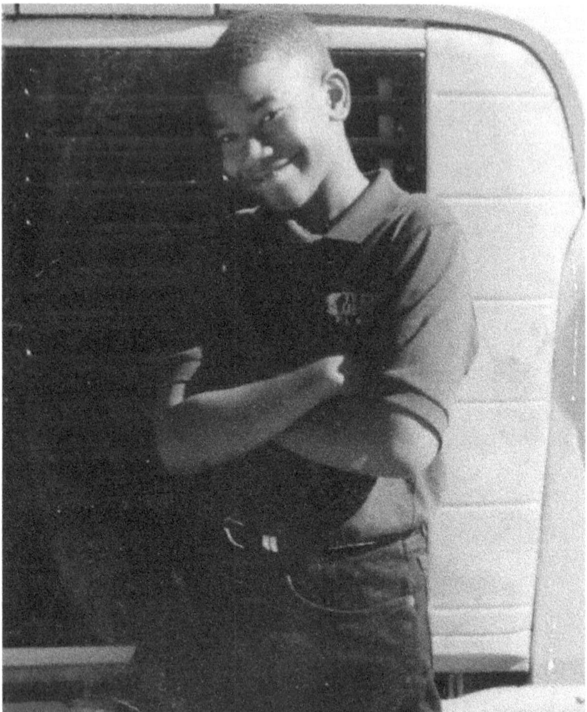

CHAPTER 6

I Wish I Knew That My Self-Worth Is Not Linked to My Achievements

> Your worth must be in who God says
> you are and not what you do!
> —Keith Collins

As I was writing this book, I came across this article that covered some of the myths associated with self-esteem. I thought that it was good information based off my own personal life experience when dealing with people. So, I included the link below so you can read the full article.
https://verilymag.com/2014/11/myths-about-low-self-esteem-debunked

Over the last couple of years, I've had the privilege of working with youth on a regular basis. One of the things I've noticed is that a lot of times they don't have a high sense of self-worth. Often, they're confidence in themselves depends on their grades, their athletic ability, their popularity, and whether they have a boyfriend or girlfriend. Yourdictionary.com defines self-worth as "the opinion you have about yourself and the value you place on yourself." An example of self-worth is your belief that you are a good person who deserves good things or your belief that you are a bad person and you deserve bad things. I find it funny that we get our self-worth from external circumstances as opposed to from internal. It's called self-worth for a reason.

At Another School, I Was an Honor Roll Student

In middle school, I was an honor roll student. That made me feel so cool because I wasn't your typical nerd. I played sports and was popular. I played football in middle school, and I ran track, but I was best at the shot put. I was on the team. Being a part of those things gave me a sense of self-worth that allowed me to walk in the hallways with a different type of swag. I could walk up to a guy and be like "Hey, you know football team …" I'd get a bit more respect than some of the other kids just because of my status. But that whole entire middle school experience only happened when I had those achievements.

During sixth and seventh grade in middle school, I was on the low end of the totem pole, and quite frankly, I was afraid of all the upperclassman because they were huge. I had no confidence in who I was. I just existed.

FATHERLESS

During eighth grade, I played all the sports and made the honor roll, which led to a trip to Washington, DC. You can see how I would have a different swagger about myself because, for once, I was on the top end of the totem pole and people knew me. That's how my self-worth grew.

My Self-Worth in Sports

My self-worth allowed me to be important based on what I did—not who I was as a person. Follow me throughout high school. In high school, I was able to be a part of various teams, including the baseball team, the football team, and the wrestling team. Being part of these teams allowed me to know many people and again have a different swagger about myself. By having friends on the outside and peers who saw me as cool, I never had to deal with who I was on the inside—the inner makings of Keith Collins.

I fell into the trap that many athletes fall into—that who they are and what they represent is limited to the sports they're involved in. It wasn't my character that made me a person who walked around with a high sense of self-worth. It was more so the abilities I had. It wasn't the fact that I was an honest, caring, and loving person that made my self-worth high; it was the fact that I was an athlete, and that's sad. We limit our self-worth to such a small standard. When those things get taken away from us, what do we have? You have yourself. That's when you have to look in the mirror and figure out who you really are, and a lot of time, people don't like who they are, so they mask and hide themselves—at least I did—in the achievements they make.

Arrogance Because I Was in College

By the time I graduated high school, it was time for college. Boy, was I excited. I was the first person in my family to go, and that truly boosted how I saw myself. Growing up in my old neighborhood, I never really experienced seeing anyone go to college, or at least they didn't mention they were in college. My parents and I moved when I was in high school, and *college* was a word I heard spoken a little bit more. So when I finally got into college, it was a badge of honor. This badge of honor soon became the thing that allowed me to start being arrogant. You might ask, "If college is a good thing, how did you become arrogant?" Let me tell you—as a student in a college, I noticed that I was a minority. That meant there were not a lot of us inside the college, let alone anywhere else I went. There just weren't a lot of black males in college. According to black demographics.com, 48 percent of black men twenty-five and older attended college in 2013, and half of them did not complete the degree program. Only 17 percent of black men have a college degree, compared to 30 percent of all men. Those are mind-boggling statistics and one of the reasons I was a little arrogant.

Don't get me wrong; this arrogance did not lead to me speaking to people harshly or anything like that, but it was one of those mental things when I thought I was better than someone else. Oftentimes when I would talk to guys in college, I would think I knew more just because I was in college. When talking with family, I used lines like "I'm in school for this here." Those things allowed me to have an ego, which is never good when leading people. Over time, I noticed this ego and started to deal with it, and it allowed me to not think of myself as better than others. I started to use a tone of gratitude. I started to realize that I was not where I was because of my own strength or ability. People blazed the path ahead of me, and my parents made sacrifices so that I would have a roof over my head and be in a home that allowed me to learn information I needed to be successful.

My Achievements as a Grown Man

Here's what I know about my achievements: they don't determine my self-worth, and they're not my own. You might ask, "But, Keith, who completed the task, completed the job?" I would say, "Me and the Lord." At this stage in my life, my character means more to me than achievements. In my earlier years, the esteem of achievement would lead me to doing things I would later regret, like cheating on tests, lying, and not giving my all. As an adult, it is more about integrity, the whole person that I am, as opposed to how I did a specific task. Here's why it matters so much—because there will be a point in my life when I have to come face-to-face with the me twenty years down the road. I want to be able to look that man in the face and be proud of his accomplishments because I know he did not compromise who he was along the way. I believe that is one of the biggest issues that happens with a lot of people who are successful; their success costs them their souls. In Mark 8:36 (NIV), it says, "What does it profit a man to gain the whole world and lose his soul?" Losing the very thing that makes you, that gives you life, your personality, is not worth gaining achievements over. Not that achievements are not important, but you can gain them the right way when you understand that success is not a onetime event. It can be who you are by understanding how to keep the core disciplines that make up your self-worth.

Origins of Self-Worth

As I mentioned, self-worth is our self-judgment or assessment of ourselves, and it can be through good or bad experiences. I do believe that sometimes our self-worth is based on a lie. There are some myths about a person with low self-worth. In a 2014 article about low self-esteem published by Verily Magazine a women's fashion and lifestyle website, there is a myth that people with low self-esteem don't think of themselves enough. That's basically untrue. The article goes on to tell us how people who think about themselves too much are those people with low self-esteem. They are so preoccupied with their own pain and disposition that they don't look at any positive aspects of their lives. The article goes on to say that there's a myth that very successful people have high self-esteem; that is untrue as well. High confidence is a blessing, and low confidence is a curse; in fact, it is the other way around, says Dr. Thomas Capasso of confidence overcoming low self-esteem, insecurity, and self-doubt. Those with low self-confidence are more sensitive to feedback, especially if it is critical or negative. Those with high self-confidence tend to be trapped by their biases of their capabilities. To prevent it from developing into missing or low self-esteem, it must be coupled with ambition and action. As you can see, there are some myths associated with our self-worth.

Self-Worth Quiz

- What is your greatest accomplishment?

- Do you get upset when you're not properly recognized?

- Have you found yourself being jealous of someone who received praise for something you did?

- Does your mood go up and down according to your academic achievements?

- What's your best character trait?

By answering these questions truthfully, you should be able to gauge where you are with your self-worth. Now the challenge is to take the information you found and do something with it—to point out to yourself when these emotions or feelings come up, to allow you to eventually get to a point where your self-worth is not determined by external forces.

Discovering Your Real Value

Ephesians 2:10 (NIV) says you are God's masterpiece, chosen in Christ anew to do great things that He planned long ago. Whether where you are at home, at work, in school, in prison, or in a car, you were created in God's image, and you're considered to be His masterpiece. When you are a masterpiece, you are the best a given artist can do. You are the thing that the artist wants to show off to the world. And when you are a piece of art, it does not matter what you say about yourself; it matters the value placed on you by your Creator.

If I were to create a work of art, no one could tell me how much it's worth. What is it worth would be whatever I say it is. Just like you. You are valuable, and your heavenly Father placed a great price on you with His son, Jesus Christ, dying on the cross for you. I don't know about you, but if someone died for me, I would be so appreciative to the point I would not know what to do with myself. But let the words that I said earlier sink into your brain: *you are God's masterpiece.* You are created in His image. You are loved more than you will ever know. No matter your background, no matter your current situation, you are loved.

Review

1. How do you view yourself?
2. Do you see yourself as a masterpiece? Why or why not? How do you evaluate your self-worth?
3. What has this chapter revealed to you about yourself?
4. What could potentially hinder you from applying some of the principles in this chapter?

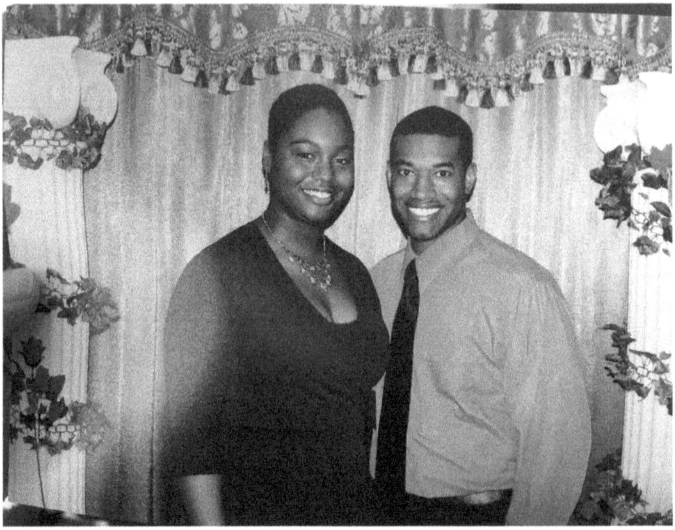

CHAPTER 7

I Wish I Knew That the Number of Girls I Could Sleep with Did Not Matter

> Being a real man doesn't mean you sleep with
> ten different women. It means you stay with one
> woman even when ten others are chasing you.
> —Unknown

Over the course of this chapter I am going to cover: some facts and stats about pornography, its effects on us as men, and proactive steps to take should we find ourselves clutched in the strong grip of pornography's hand.

Listed below I included the link to some of the research I have found on the effects of pornography. I also include

a link filled with steps to help you change any unwanted behavior you may have in your life.
https://www.telegraph.co.uk/men/thinking-man/scary-effects-pornography-21st-centurys-accute-addiction-rewiring/
https://knowhownonprofit.org/people/people-management-skills/change/basics-on-managing-change/fivesteps

How does a young boy get considered to be a man? This was the question that I thought I knew the answer to at a young age. In my neighborhood, I always heard the older boys talk about the girls they were able to have sex with. This was around middle school age for me, and it started to build up the whole I-can't-wait-to-have-sex mentality. What I failed to realize is that some of the guys who talked about having sex were probably lying.

Over the next couple of pages, I'm going to explore the mistakes I made growing up as a young boy in the area of sexual relations. I want to make it known that I'm not glorifying what I did; I'm just speaking to my life experiences so that it can help you, no matter your level of expertise, to challenge yourself to be better than you are today. And to be honest with you, it's going to take hard work.

Introduction to Pornography

When I was in middle school, one day I stumbled across my uncle's *Playboy* collection. This was an eye-opening discovery for me. At the time, I had only heard about what a woman looks like naked and the things that women do in the bedroom. I can remember every so often when my parents were away, sneaking into the closet to gain a peek at pictures to try to keep the image embedded in my brain.

In middle school, the desire to see X-rated material increased, and it led to me finding DVDs and videos in my home and occasionally going home after school and watching them. It's crazy how at a young age, although I found myself experiencing pleasure while watching the videos, afterward I always had a sense of guilt. I did not understand the emotional toll it was taking on me. I just knew if I waited a couple of days, the guilt would subside, and I would be back at searching for the next images to store up in my brain.

In a study from the *Telegraph* newspaper titled "The Scary Effects of Pornography," it talked about the ever-growing industry of pornography and its effects. In 2014, a Cambridge University study found that pornography triggers brain activity in sex addicts in the same way drugs trigger drug addicts. The article goes on to say compulsive behaviors, including watching porn, are increasingly common. A study by researchers at the University of California found a rare positive correlation between porn and watching the libido; the consensus is on the opposite side. The article also goes on to talk about how excessive porn usage is linked to erectile dysfunction in young men. And there's a whole host of effects that pornography has on relationships, and I'm not going to get into it at this time. What I do know is that in middle school, I wish I knew its toxic effects—before it followed me through high school.

Lust in My Heart

When I entered high school, I had a pretty good idea what sex was. It wasn't something that I was looking to have, but it did not stop me from looking at the opposite sex as if they had something I wanted. Keep in mind that this lesser desire only grew with my constant seeking of X-rated content. For some reason, in high school, it seemed as if kids were no longer just all talk about their sexual experiences. It seemed as if I was the only one who hadn't had sex. Although that might not be true, it sure did feel like it.

It's crazy how lust, over time, changed my perspective on sex. At one point, I held it as something to be sacred for marriage. I remember at one point in high school having a girlfriend who wanted to have sex, and she told me she was a virgin. I consciously could not put myself to taking that from her, and I respectfully declined the opportunity to have sex with her. Then a switch went off entering my senior year of high school. I made it a personal goal to not be the only one not having sex.

During this time, I remember having a girlfriend who had already had sex, and she was going to allow me to partake in the experience with her, and we did. It continued throughout my senior year and basically opened Pandora's box. Over the next couple of years, I would have many other sexual partners, with no full commitment to the relationship. It was more recreational. Upon entering college, I got into a more fully committed relationship, but I still had sex on the brain.

When I got to college, I got in a real, committed relationship, and what that meant for me was I could have sex anytime I wanted to. Don't get me wrong, I had feelings for them only, and that grew over time, but initially it was more of a physical attraction, and it developed into more than just physical. I remember different points within the relationship and my quest to make the relationship more intimate in terms of having a deeper connection with my girlfriend. I would practice abstinence to see how much closer we could draw to each other. These attempts would last for a week or a month, and then it continued.

One of the crazy things was that during this stage in my life, I was growing my relationship with God, and I started to feel convicted for the things I was doing. On Sunday, I would be praising God and tithing and trying to draw closer to Him, and throughout the week, I would be living in sin. I will be the first one to tell you that there comes a point when you have to sacrifice your old you to get to your new you. This was the time of my life when I started to make a more conscious decision to try to live up to the standards that God had place for me, and eventually God started working in my life even more.

As I started to reflect more on what God was doing inside of me, people started to notice, and some of my coworkers even made statements about how they were happy that I found God because my old self had some issues. I must say they were things that I did not want to take into my marriage.

It All Affects My Marriage

Just because I did not want to take some of my previous sins into my marriage does not mean they did not come with me. And the stuff that did come with me affected my marriage.

When I first got married, I had to deal with the issue of lust and the conviction I felt when I sometimes would look at a girl twice. I also had to deal with the feelings or emotions of wanting to fall back into my old ways, before I started to try to walk the straight line in terms of pornography and other sexual sins.

To this day, I still struggle with the desires of my old ways, but I've been married for six years and have two beautiful sons who I do not want to experience the pain that I had to experience through my sexual sin. So now I have a why that keeps me grounded in terms of trying to achieve sexual and mental pureness. My biggest hope as a father is that I can guide them down a path that will protect them from pornography and sexual sin.

Myths about Proving Your Manhood

There are two major myths in reference to how to determine a man's manhood. One is that the way you show that you are a man is the number of girls you sleep with. The other method is as long as the sex is good, it does not matter what the relationship is like. These two myths could not be further from the truth.

When you think about the idea that the more girls you sleep with, the more of a man you are, it's pretty sad. It implies that only sexual activity makes you a man. It also implies that it's a competition, as if you're back in grade school. When we take on this ideology, it hinders us from being in real and authentic relationships that lead to healthy and stable marriages. It also screws up our perception of women, and they become more objectified. They become more like trophies that we hang up on the wall as if we were hunters. This is not the image we should portray to the young men who are coming behind us.

Sex cannot be the end goal in a relationship. Relationships take hard work, and if sex is the only thing holding a relationship together, the relationship is very surface level. There is no true intimacy that creates growth that will continue to produce longevity in the relationship, whether married or single. Don't get me wrong; sex is good, but it was meant to be enjoyed in the confines of marriage. When we have sex before marriage, we mess with God's original intent for humankind. This means that we step outside of the boundaries, which leads to hurt and consequences. So, why does this all matter?

Why Does It Matter?

The hard truth is this: when we do not do male and female relationships the way in which God intended, we do not receive the fullness of His promise. It's like Pastor Troy Gramling says: the enemy—being Satan—tempts us with whipped cream, when God has designed us to have the whole cheesecake with the whipped cream. You settle before being able to receive the very best of what God has for you.

When a man and woman have sex, it's like a spiritual operation is performed, and the two become one flesh. If at any given point the man and woman split up, it's like trying to cut in half something that was once one; that's why there's so much pain involved. This pain is felt at different levels, whether it's a boyfriend-girlfriend relationship or a husband and wife. Pain hurts and demands to be felt. This is one of the reasons I say, if you are a man and woman living together, you should get separate places to live or get married. You might have many excuses when you hear a statement like that, but I want to challenge you to test God in this matter and allow Him to bless your marriage when done the proper way.

I once had a couple serving in my ministry who lived together and had a child. I found out that they were not married and began the process of challenging them to make the commitment to each other. Over time, the boyfriend's heart began to soften for the things of God, and it led to him confessing his faith to the world through baptism. And then it led to him and his girlfriend getting married. Then God opened up the windows of heaven on their lives. They had their second child, and then the husband opened up a business, and it is still thriving to this day. I do believe that when we are obedient to the things that God has asked us, it sets us up for supernatural blessings that can only be reached through proper obedience.

How to Course Correct

After reading this chapter, you might be at a point where you are looking to course correct. Well, you have come to the right person. I want to give you five steps to change any situation. In an article published by nohownonprofit.org, it gives us five steps to successful change. Here's the list:

- Know and understand the need for change. If we are all honest with ourselves, no one can help anyone who is not willing to admit that they need help.

- Communicate the need and involve people in developing the change. This is where we start to develop accountability partners that will help us with our sexual sins and just sins in general.

- Develop changed plans. This is where you start to develop new behaviors that will keep you from falling into the trap of sexual sins, so this could be something like running, basketball, and video games.

- As you develop a plan, you must implement it. Plans are just hopes and ideas if we do not implement them. There's no way to validate if we do not implement them.

- Evaluate progress and celebrate success. We all love to succeed. One of the surefire ways to succeed is to evaluate your experiences to help benefit and better your current condition.

Review

1. What makes up a man?
2. What was a key insight that you took away from this chapter?
3. What are some other myths that you grew up believing as a young boy?

4. How can you protect your family from the effects of pornography?
5. What do you need to stop doing, or start doing, in regard to the opposite sex?

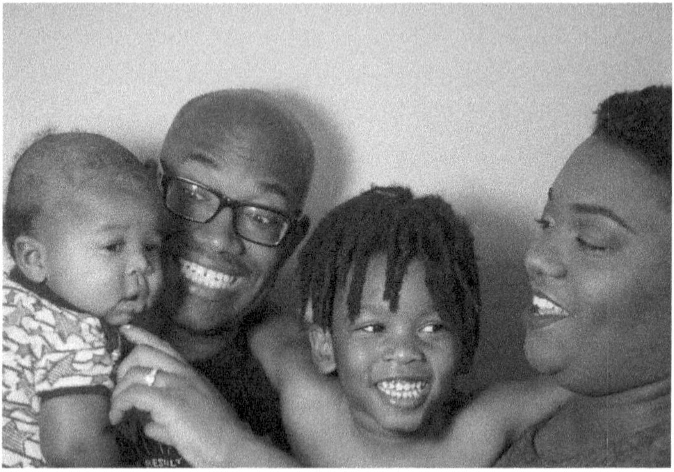

CHAPTER 8

I Wish I Knew That Being Male Came with So Much Responsibility

> The real man smiles in trouble, gathers strength
> from distress, and grows brave by reflection.
> —Thomas Paine

I'm not going to lie to you. Being a guy is so much fun. First off, you're pretty fast, you don't have to give a perfect toe touch, and you can pretty much pee anywhere. Don't get me wrong. I'm not chauvinistic. I respect the women in my life. In fact, I respect my wife to the utmost. I've watched her give birth in a birthing center to my oldest son and also inside of the hospital. I watched her in the course of a month get a real estate license all while being on maternity leave. So, I know the value of women and the roles they play. The only thing I did not know at the rightful age of thirty is how much responsibility is laid upon a man. When I think of this, I think of the context of the social aspect, where you are considered the main breadwinner, and then also the biblical aspect, where you are considered the head of the house. These two pressures alone will make any man concerned.

Chores in Middle School

In middle school, I was given the honor of washing dishes, keeping my room clean, and doing any of the chores deemed necessary by my parents. That's a lot growing up. I did not want to clean my room. In fact, the mere thought of cleaning my room calls me to have a headache. I can still see the stacks of clothes piled up in one area of my room, and then I would clean it only when my mom said I couldn't go outside. Fast-forward now at thirty, and it still seems that way in my house with my wife.

I have this place called the drop spot. It's a place where, when I take off my stuff, I can just drop it there. This helps me because I have a place where I can release everything that weighed me down for the day. The unfortunate part is that it piles up like a huge mountain of trash. I do clean it up at least once a week … okay, once every three weeks. But it's one of the responsibilities that I have around the house. This was one that I wished I could have learned when I was younger.

As I mentioned earlier, when I was younger in middle school, I had chores. I really did not take them seriously and did not understand the long-term ramifications they would have on my life. I didn't understand how they were going to help me become a better person. I grew up, I slowly began to understand and realize the value and the responsibility that I had.

I Led the Relationship with Girls

As I mentioned in a previous chapter, when I was in high school, I was really into girls. What I did not understand or realize was how much I affected the relationship. When I think back over my relationships, I can now see how, as the guy, I determined a lot.

As a guy in a relationship, I had a great influence on where we would go. Many times I was good at giving directions, so when it was time to go out on a date, I would drive and take the girl where I had in mind. This gave me control over how the night would go in terms of what movie we would watch and where we would go and eat. All those things were arranged by me because I was paying and driving. I also learned that I controlled the conversation.

I remember in high school having late-night phone calls with different girls. In the midst of those conversations with the girls, I would often steer the conversation in a new direction that I wanted it to go. That's not to say that girls do not have any control in the relationship, but a lot of times, based on our society, many girls or young ladies do not have strong male figures in their lives. So when I was a guy taking interest in a girl, I had great influence on the young lady because there was a lack of a male figure in the girl's life. This means that they were more willing to do things or go with the flow because I was that male that was in their life at the time. I remember dating a girl who could not carry on a conversation, and when we were on the phone, it was more of just me listening to her breathing. That led me to break up with her. I remember the frustration I had, the feeling that I had to always carry the conversation, and it was not fun for me at the time because I wanted to hear her talk sweet nothings in my ear. But that all changed as I entered college.

I Impact Society

To be honest with you, when I was in college, I did not understand fully the measure of my impact as a male. Something was happening in society and cultural trends, but I did not put my finger on the fact that, as a man, I get to change society. Eventually, I started to gain some impact, toward my senior year of college, when I wanted to give back to society. It all started when I was involved in a multilevel marketing book group called Amway.

I spent a lot of time around people who were considered to be my mentors. These were men who were successful in life and were multimillionaires. One guy who impacted me the most was a guy named Greg Francis. He talked about how other men need to be encouraged, challenged, and told that they are men. He found this out through reading a book called *Wild at Heart*.

As mentioned earlier, *Wild at Heart* by John Eldridge radically changed my life. In this book, I discovered my passion to see other young men succeed in life. This book encouraged me to give back. One of the things I was able to do was volunteer at a boys' group home, and serving there eventually led to working there for year. Those two years, I discovered that I had a pastor's heart. I found myself engaging in good conversation with the young men and eventually ended up teaching them in Bible study format about the Bible. That led to me having a desire to, at some point in my life, teach in a church setting. I did not know how that was going to happen, but I knew once I moved to Florida, at some point I would step into ministry, which would ultimately start the process of me impacting society.

I Affect Generations

After I moved to Florida, I continued to serve my community through the local church. I started volunteering in the youth ministry, and that led me to become a staff member. It is a place I still serve today. My favorite part about being involved in youth ministry is the fact that I get to make a generational impact on many parents and students, which transcends generations.

In addition to serving at the church, God has blessed me with two children. I have a four-year-old and a five-month-old. The Creator of the entire universe entrusted me to be the father of these two young children—which is exciting because, as I said earlier, I believe everything rises and falls on the male leadership in the household. So what a great opportunity I have to impact the next generation through my sons. I think of some of the things that I went through, and I know I do not have to pass on those experiences to them. I was a part of my children's births, and I was able to cut the umbilical cord. I was able to watch them take their first steps and hear them say their first words. I have also been there for some of those disciplinary moments with the toddler. The point of it all is that there's no way you can tell me that I am not a generational influence. They say that the average person comes across ten thousand people in the span of their life, and as I sit back and think about the people I get to impact—whether it's the hundreds of students throughout the course of the weekend, with the thousands of parents when I have an opportunity to share inside of our main auditorium at our church, then multiply that times tens of thousands—I'm literally doing something that I never even knew I could do. That's the generational impact, and it is a role that is called upon all fathers.

Proverbs 13:22 (NIV) says a godly man leaves an inheritance for his children's children. When I think about this scriptural reference, I think that my being on earth does have a final word. It has an impact on all of society. Just being a man changes the course of relationships, society, and families. I did not know it would be tons of responsibility, but I have discovered that through a relationship with Christ and His Word, the Bible, I have the tools to make the most of the opportunity and to leave a mark upon the next generation.

Relationships

As a male, I play a pivotal role in the crafting of a successful marriage. I have the ability to fan the flames of communication, anger, and home stability.

When I first got married, I was not the best of communicators. To be honest, I am still working on my communication skills. The first years of our marriage, my wife would say something to me, and I would not really take it to heart or try to understand what she was really saying. She would say something like, "I would love to go there to eat one day and just hang out. I think it would be an awesome place to spend time together." I took it as *I'm not doing anything, and I need to do more for her.*

Slowly, as our relationship began to grow, I understood that she was saying she wanted to spend time with me, and she was dropping a hint of a place that would be awesome for us to go out to dinner.

Now, she didn't always drop hints. There was a good season when I felt like I was on a game show. I had to guess with charades what she was trying to say. She would make so many hypotheticals and automatically assume that I knew what she was talking about, so when I did not perform to her expectation, it led to frustration. And that frustration led to anger in the relationship.

Of course, as a man, when I was unable to keep my wife happy, it led to me being frustrated, which led me to become more secluded in terms of my communication, which turned into anger. I would find myself being upset with my wife without her even knowing it, because of an inability to get myself right to actually listen to what she was asking me for. After a call one time, I got super upset and frustrated with our relationship and our current state. I prayed and asked God for help and understanding. Often, He would give me the answer, but I would soon forget and slide back into my pattern.

As a man, when you find yourself in a rut and you see the light, it often frustrates you, and this frustration changes the whole course of the marriage. That's why it's so important. To maintain a close relationship with God, He's going to work on you while you spend time with Him. There were some practical things I did to improve my relationship so I wouldn't be so angry when I failed to meet my wife's expectations—or my own expectations for that matter. I started to write things down on a calendar. I started to remember important dates and planned ahead. I also took the initiative to set a goal for how many times I wanted to be on a date with my wife. All of those things helped me improve the relationship, which allowed for me and my wife to grow closer, and it ultimately led to us having a happy and fulfilled marriage. I'm not saying we don't have disagreements, but they are few and far in between. I believe it is because, as a man, I took sole responsibility for the home and for the relationship between me and my wife—and I'm happy I know that now.

Spiritual

In Genesis, it speaks about how God created man in his image, to dwell and have dominion over the earth (Genesis 1:26 NIV). Dominion means to have ownership or rule, to be like the Creator God. When Adam and Eve sinned in the Garden of Eden, God went to Adam. Adam was not ready for the responsibility and blamed God for giving him the woman. So, as you can see, starting off, man passed off the responsibility that God had given him.

As men, when we pass off responsibility for the family to others, we don't show children the proper order that God set in place long ago. In essence, we disrupt the plan that God originally set up. Remember it's our responsibility to seek to be the head of the household, which means to lead, guide, and protect the family in the way in which God wants us to. I think it is in Joshua 24:15 (NIV) that it says, "As for me and my house, we will serve the Lord." That comes from a conscious decision, knowing who your Creator is and the role and responsibility He has placed in your life. Truthfully, it means taking ownership—taking ownership for your kids, for your wife, and for all of those responsibilities man received.

In the New Testament, the writer Paul say in 1 Corinthians 11:3 (NIV), "The head of Christ is God, and Christ is the head of the man, and the man is the head of the household." As you can see, God set up authority for the male back in the time of Adam, and it still continues to this day. What has caused us as men to neglect this spiritual responsibility?

If we were to be honest with ourselves as men, we can't lead our families until we are led by Christ. This means growing ourselves to have a good relationship so we can understand His heart. God wants us to have a deep relationship with Him. We can get a strong sense of this as we read God's Word in the Bible on a daily basis. Yes, I said it—read God's Word on a daily basis. That's one of the ways that you and I can protect our families from a lot of the things that are going on in this world. As we do the same, we model it for our families—that we are not above being a follower. That allows them to follow us.

As we take back our rightful place as head of the household in a relationship with Jesus, our families will be restored and transformed because we have taken the responsibility of being males seriously. I'm happy that I know this now.

From a societal standpoint, our role as men is to be leaders. When you think about most facets of our civilization, men are considered the leaders. This is not saying that women are not leaders. But from a natural sense, men are looked at as leaders. And there's nothing wrong with that. I do believe going forward we have to lead with a sense of grace and excessive understanding. I am convinced that, as we take our roles as leaders seriously, it can change the work environment, the social aspect, and our homes.

I believe we should constantly be growing in our leadership, learning new ways to communicate better, finding ways to connect better, and finding ways to empathize better. These are critical components that will help us to be more effective in the workplace and inside our homes. Until we're able to do these things, the environment we have been given will suffer. I'm not down for suffering, which is one of the reasons I wrote this book.

Review

1. What responsibility do you feel you were not ready for as a male? Why?
2. How have you learned to deal with that responsibility?
3. In what ways have you started to stretch yourself spiritually?
4. Would your family consider you to be the leader in the house? Why or why not?
5. What steps can you take today to step into the responsibility you've been given?

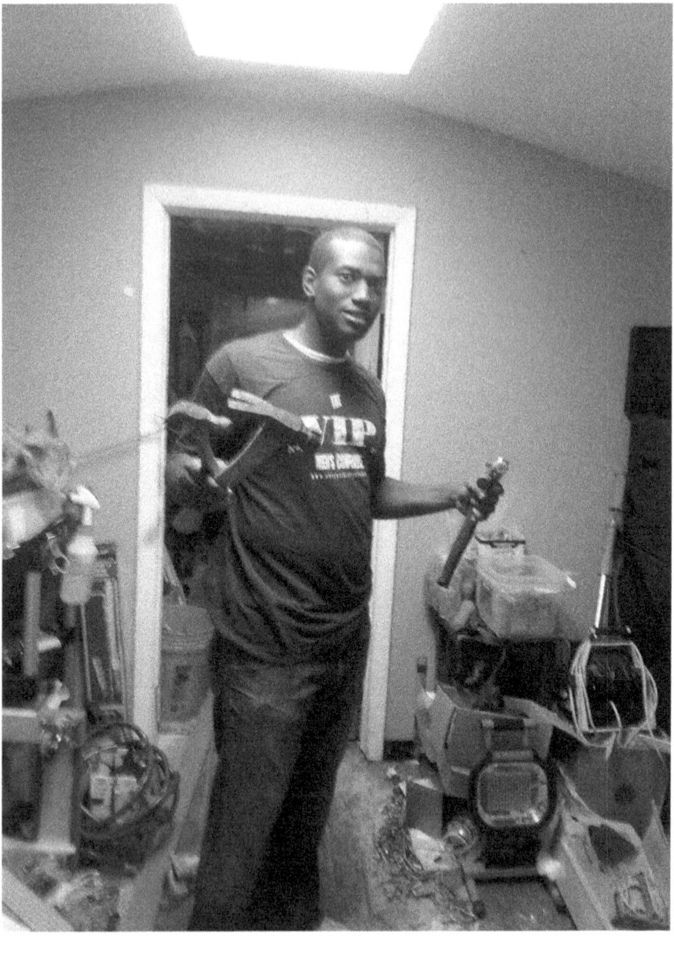
VIP

CHAPTER 9

I Wish I Knew the Value of Mentorship

> One of the greatest values of mentors is the ability to see ahead what others cannot see and to help them navigate a course to their destination.
> —John C. Maxwell

"I think I got this." These words are commonly said, but we often need the help of others. I'm not talking about the work aspect. What really matters in how to navigate in the house is are we a great husband, a great father, or overall just a leader who practices self-control. These are more vulnerable areas in a man's life, and we often don't have people pointing us in the right direction. What I found is that mentors allow us to grow exponentially when it comes to reaching all that God has for us. I wish that when I was younger, I understood the value of mentoring.

No Thoughts of It

When I was in middle school, I had no thoughts of getting mentorship. I only thought about making friends—new friends, that is. Entering into a new school, I did not think about seeking the upperclassmen to show me the ropes and how to navigate classrooms, teachers, or social groups within the school. I took on a lot of those experiences by trial and error, which I will admit can be one of the hardest things to do. I could have used my middle school time to avoid certain hurdles. In middle school, my thought process was not long-term; it was more in the moment.

I remember associating with guys who always got together during lunch and made fun of others. I did not know how immature this was—to spend our entire lunch laughing at others' imperfections. Keep in mind it was in middle school and there was a lot of pressure.

I wish that in middle school I had taken the time to grasp what mentorship could do for me in those social settings. The closest thing I had to a mentor was my cousin Antonio. He was a few grades above me, and our relationship transformed my middle school experience. He encouraged me to play football and do well in school, but I did not think of it as mentorship. I thought it was just someone having my back. I guess you could say that was the start of me having mentorship in my life.

I Learned a Little through High School Wrestling

In high school, I didn't think through the whole concept of finding someone to guide me. When I think back, I would say that person was the guidance counselor. I remember going to figure out what classes I needed to take in order to get out of school as quickly as possible.

High school was more like *every man for himself*. I did not seek the advice of the upperclassmen in the beginning, and I did not care about the other classes until I got to eleventh and twelfth grade; that's when I cared about the underclassmen below me. I just wanted to make sure that I did not treat them like the low man on the totem pole and actually gave them respect. But when I think about mentorship and learning and using it to grow, I remember really focusing in on it during my eleventh- and twelfth-grade years.

I remember my first year of wrestling and not taking advantage of practicing with the guys who had wrestled way longer than I had. I was intimidated because someone went to state or played in the finals that year. I could've taken that as an opportunity to try to learn from them and then get better, to shorten my learning curve. I could have used the time to improve my mind-set about what I was capable of and the potential I had inside of me. Instead, I played this mental game, *I'm not as good as these guys*, which meant that if I said I needed help, I would be considered weak. To sum it up, I was insecure.

My second year in wrestling was my senior year, and that was the year I decided to find a mentor. I created a system in my head that would allow me to get better in practice, so it would later produce better results on the mat. I found myself working out with some of those who were more experienced. You might see it inside of your work environment or your school environment with people who are considered the top in the field, who would associate with other people in their field. Often, insecurities stop people like you and me from ever raising our hand and asking for help. In actuality, people who are doing well or in the top of their field love sharing knowledge and helping others around them, because they understand that someone once helped them, which allowed them to be where they are in life. So, back to me and wrestling. I would intentionally wrestle one of our quicker teammates just so I could gain mentorship on being quick and understand the mind-set of a quick opponent. Because I was larger than the lighter opponents, there were certain things they would do to expose weak areas in me. I also wrestled with people who were better than me, because they would explore their strengths, which allowed me to get stronger and learn how to exploit the weaknesses of a larger, stronger opponent. Wrestling with these various levels helped me to grow my second year, and that was one of the components that led to getting one win away from making it to the state tournament.

In College, I Learned the Truth about Mentorship

Upon entering into college, I still did not really grasp the whole concept of mentorship. In fact, I thought it was just a buzzword. I would hear someone say, "Yeah, I got a mentor," or "My mentor said …"

Upon entering college, I got involved in a multilevel marketing business. I was exposed to great men and women who had qualities in their lives that I wanted. I met people who were faithful to the wise, successful in business, and overall good people. During this time, I received countless bits of wisdom that dealt with my relationship and allowed me to have a successful setup for marriage because of the accountability given to me.

I also became a mentor during this time. At work, I was promoted multiple times and was given charge of developing leaders. This was a huge responsibility I had been given—one that I was proud of. Because I was able to succeed, I was excited to give back to others and help them get to where I was able to, while avoiding some of the pitfalls and mistakes I had already made. I truly believe that great mentors help their mentees experience life in a way that doesn't allow life to beat them up. Ultimately, it starts growth that the mentee would not have received otherwise. I felt that it was something I was offering the people that I was leading, and it showed. During that season of life, I was able to produce countless people who are deemed credible leaders in our workplace.

I also received mentorship in school and college. I was able to connect with teachers all throughout my different courses who would play a vital role in me finding a job, navigating school, and ultimately being successful. These teachers made it easy for me to transition from the academic world into the workforce and ultimately into adulthood.

Now as an adult, I see mentorship differently.

After I left home in Georgia, upon graduating from college, I started to understand that I could receive mentorship in different ways. I could receive mentorship through books, podcasts, YouTube, and other platforms. I had always thought that mentorship had to be a physical person sitting down with me over a cup of coffee, but as I became a man, I understood that I could learn from any person, at any time, in any situation. So, there is a group of people who mentor me who do not even know it.

This new understanding allowed me to see life differently and assess my life in different ways. When I first moved to Florida, I worked at a company and then transitioned from that company because of something one of my mentors said. My mentor was a guy by the name of John Maxwell. He is an author and a speaker, and one of the things that he said was, I can tell where you are going to be in the next five years by the people you associate with and the books you read. This was a mind-blowing statement to me, and I used it to help me navigate different scenarios and life situations. I left my first job in Florida because I looked at the example that was set before me, and I saw that it was not what I wanted for my life.

Having mentorship alone does not automatically produce change in my life. There has to be a will for me—the desire to grow. This unquenchable desire to grow is something that will have to sustain me through the process of pain. My favorite motivational speaker, Eric Thomas, said, "I use the pain to push me to greatness … let me say that again, I used the pain to push me to greatness." He also says, "You're already in pain; you might as well get a reward from it. Don't cry to give up. Cry to keep going." Mentorship like that has allowed me to grow into the amazing young man that I am today. I want you to take what I have learned about mentorship and apply it to your life. Find that person who's going to help mold you to be even better than they were in their life.

As a man, it is important for us to seek mentorship, to have mentors in our lives. These mentors help us to grow past our self-limiting beliefs. These mentors help us to stretch farther than we ever thought possible. Lastly, we help our mentors be able to leave this life not having robbed from but deposited into it. In the words of Myles Monroe, "If you leave this earth and make no major contribution, you are a generational thief." I know that's not you, and I know that's not me.

Pros and Cons of Mentorship

As with anything, there are pros and cons to seeking mentorship. I want to look at the effects of mentorship. Hopefully, this will allow you to see what decisions you need to make to see if mentorship is right for you. I do believe this will help you to make a more educated decision.

When you have a mentor, you grow as a person. You might say, "So, Keith, I've grown no matter what!" That's true, but the question is, Are you growing closer to your dream, or are you going farther away from it? Growth of something does happen automatically, but you must make a conscious effort to grow whatever it is you desire in your life, whether it be a better father, a better husband, or a better leader. Your growth depends on being intentional, seeking people who are going to grow you. As I have learned the value of mentorship, I have grown tremendously. The growth isn't something you can necessarily see physically, as it starts from within. There's a story about a Chinese bamboo tree. For the bamboo tree to grow and reach one hundred feet tall, the seed must be watered every day for a total of five years. The first couple of years, about four or so, you see no growth from the tree. Suddenly, in the fifth year, the tree grows to be one hundred feet tall. Now the question is, Does the tree grow one hundred feet tall in one year or five years? The answer is obviously five years, and that's the same thing that happens to us. When we seek mentorship, growth happens, and we don't see it all at one time. So if you want to grow as a person, it's going to require you return to the generation either in front of you or behind you and seek mentorship.

Another pro that comes with seeking mentorship is that you get feedback. Now feedback is not a term we hear a lot, but it means anytime someone lets you know something about yourself—whether positive or negative. I learned in college that there is no negative criticism or positive criticism; it is all just feedback. And when you partake in having a mentor, you get a constant flow of feedback, which allows you to grow in phenomenal ways. By receiving feedback, you are able to learn from your mistakes and make better future decisions, which ultimately gets you closer to your goal or dream. Here's a quick side note: as a man, it's very easy to rely on egos to get in the way of receiving feedback. So, be aware of this.

As you receive feedback from your mentor, try your best not to get defensive. When we are defensive, that just means we are scared, and that just means we are insecure. Did I just say you're insecure? Yes—but the truth is truth. And I'm willing to say whatever I need to say to get through to you because I care that much about you and the legacy that you leave on this earth. So be willing to step into the feedback that you receive as you grow to become the best version of yourself you can be.

The only con is that I will have to change. You might say, "Keith, that's the con of mentorship?" Yes it is. You will be forced—or encouraged—to change from your old you to get to your new you. This change will stretch you, and that stretching is where pain is. As I said earlier, use your pain to push you to greatness.

How to Find a Good Mentor

There are many ways to find a good mentor. I want to suggest the one that has been most effective in my growth and development. The one surefire way to find a great mentor is to look for qualities that you would like to have and then learn from that person. So, you will not just have one mentor who will guide you through your life. I suggest finding multiple mentors. Everyone has something we can learn from them, and in the case of finding a great mentor, the person you find might not have everything you want. If I wanted to learn about real estate, I would find someone who specializes in the area of real estate. If I wanted to become a better dad, I'd find a man who has had some success raising his kids and spend time learning from him.

As you discover who your mentor is, I suggest putting your mentor on a trial run to see if the relationship will last and be sustained for a long period. If it does not last, that's okay. One thing I know about seasons is they do change—well, unless you live in South Florida. Then the season never changes. But in all seriousness, when finding a mentor, it's never a one-stop shop, so know that and embrace it because your destiny is on the other side.

I wish I could communicate to you how important it is to seek mentorship and appreciate its value. Here's why it's important: your future, your kids' future, your boss's future, society, and relationships all depend on it!

Review

1. What stood out to you in this chapter?
2. When did you first hear the word mentorship?
3. Who is a current mentor in your life?
4. What experience have you had with mentorship?
5. What keeps us from seeking mentorship, and how can we deal with it?

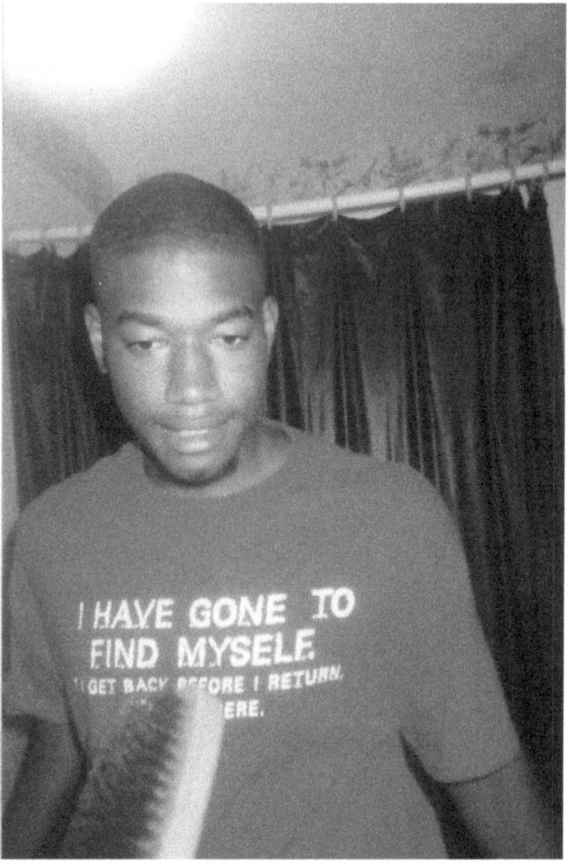
I HAVE GONE TO
FIND MYSELF

CHAPTER 10

I Wish I Knew That Reading Would Change My World

The book you don't read won't help.
—Jim Rohn

"Leaders are readers" is a quote I've often heard. But let's be honest. Who really wants to read? I'm assuming you like to read because you're reading the words on this page. But for many of us, reading is not fun; it's not something that we go home screaming we should do. Reading was one of those things that you did because the teacher told you to do it, and when you became older, you vowed to never do it again. At least that's what I thought. It wasn't until college that it changed for me. I eventually figured some things out.

I Started as an Okay Reader

My middle school years were plagued with insecurities and so much self-consciousness. When it came to the time to read in class, I always was nervous. Think about a kid whose heart started pounding as if he were about to suffer cardiac arrest—that was me. I never considered myself to be a strong reader, but in middle school, I don't think I was considered to be a weak reader. I could talk all day, but when it was time to read, I was quiet as a mouse. Oftentimes, I was in the classroom and did not even make eye contact with anyone around me. We used to do this thing called popcorn reading in class—and man, did I hate it. Here's how it went down. One person started reading in the classroom, and at some point, the person would stop reading and call, "Popcorn!" and then call on another person to read. This sent chills up my spine. The teacher would do it, or a student would, and the student would sometimes use it as an opportunity to pick on people who couldn't read super strong—which was me. I dreaded the reading time in class, every aching minute—even if it was only for thirty minutes. I did not appreciate reading or books because it struck so much fear inside of me, and I didn't understand the importance of doing it on a consistent basis. In high school, I started to grab hold of the information from reading, and it led me to doing better.

I Got Better at Reading

In high school, I did pretty well in language arts class. In fact, I got as far as being a part of the honors literature class. I think it just meant I had to read more than other students, as opposed to meaning that I was some special kid. I do remember having to read a lot of Shakespeare. But it was all good because the teacher did not make us popcorn read in class. In high school, I started to read on my own time and did not have to worry about the classroom social pressure or the anxiety that often came along with reading. I used the time reading at home to grow into a more solid reader. I focused on learning how to retain the information in my memory bank for a later time. This was important because there were tests I had to take that would challenge my ability to comprehend the information that was given to me in a particular paragraph at a given time. My high school prepared me for life.

I then started reading books that helped me grow.

I think most kids do not enjoy reading too much. But over time, dabbling in books, I finally found something I started to enjoy. I enjoy self-help books. In college, I started to discover them, and it opened me to up a whole new world of possibilities that would help me grow as a person. I believe the reason students don't read as much is they don't see their parents doing it, and they use force to get their children to read material that is uninteresting or feels irrelevant. Growing up, I don't recall any of my parents reading for the sake of growth, outside of my dad. He was a Jehovah's Witness, and I recall him reading a line of *Watchtower* publications. So I guess you can say I did see someone read a lot.

In college, my love for reading peaked when I started to grow as a person. You've heard me say it before, but the growth that you desire to reach first happens from within, before you see it manifest on the outside, and that's exactly what happened to me. During college, I was involved with

Amway and was encouraged to read on a consistent basis. That taught me that reading should be consistent. I was also told that a book should never defeat you. I was told you never can get mad at a book because books reveal truth, and truth reveals who you are, and you can only change or get mad. A book can challenge you, but you can't punch the book; you can only put it down. In college, that's exactly what I did. I accepted the challenge. And by accepting that challenge long ago, I was able to take a lot of the growth and apply it to adulthood.

I Have an Addiction

Hi, my name is Keith, and I am a readaholic. That's a new word I came up with. I do enjoy a good book. You might ask yourself, "Why in the world would I want to do that?" You can take a person's life and gain tons of insight that can guide you so you don't have to make the same mistakes they made, or you can see how it applies to your life. All of this information is found in a ten-dollar book. A person's entire life can be compressed into a book of about two hundred pages.

I set goals every year for how many books I would like to read. Sometimes I fall short of those goals, but I'm striving to read as much as possible. This reading as much as possible sometimes gets on my wife's nerves, because I find myself buying books any chance I get. I am a firm believer that leaders are readers. Do I consider myself a leader? I guess that means I must. I don't know where you are in the grand scheme of this reading thing, but I can encourage you that the more you read, the more you will learn to enjoy it. I also will go ahead and say never let a book defeat you. Never give up on a book you start; you can gain something from it even if you find it on the last page. You never know if what you learned can radically change your life.

When I first started reading, I posed the question, Why should I read? And if you're one of those people, I pose a question also: Why not invest in yourself? In a nutshell, that's exactly what reading is, an investment in your future. It is an investment in who you are, an investment in the future generations. Reading can save you time and money that you would spend learning through the school of hard knocks. That's one of the reasons I'm writing this book, so that you can learn from my mistakes, so you do not have to experience the same pains and heartache that I had to experience because I was not willing to step in and read. Listen, whether or not you pick up another book is completely up to you. I just hope that you understand the value of reading enough to invest in your future. And if it's reading physically that's not the thing for you, my next suggestion would be audiobooks. It's like listening to the radio—without the commercials.

In a book called *The Slight Edge*, there is a story about a lady who was looking to raise money for her daughter to go to cheerleading camp. The mother worked in the airport and shined shoes, and she had a huge stack of romance novels close to her booth. The author poses the question, What if the mother spent the same amount of time reading books that would grow her and develop her personally as she spent reading those romance novels? What would the outcome be? Would she be working at the airport shining shoes? Would she even need to ask for money? Would she have built up a wealth of knowledge that would allow her to change her circumstances? Malcolm Gladwell, in his book *Outliers*, says when we put ten thousand hours into a given subject, we become experts. What would it look like to pick up a book or audiobook and commit to spending one hour a day to learning and growing in your craft? How would that dramatically change your life?

Why People Don't Read

I believe the two biggest reasons people do not read is that they're distracted and they don't see immediate change.

There is so much in this world that is grabbing our attention on any given day. From social media to TV to everyday worries and fears, all of them grab for attention and take away from the time that we could use doing something other than mindlessly thumbing through our phones or worrying about a future outcome that will probably not happen. Distraction is one of the biggest tools of the enemy. Distractions keep us from focusing, and just like a lion inside of the cage with a lion tamer, we sometimes can get distracted, which keeps us off track. In case you didn't know, that's one of the reasons that lion tamers in the earlier days would use stools to distract lions and tigers, because the stools had four legs, and the lion would try to focus on all four legs at one time and then would be paralyzed. That's what happens in our lives. We try to focus on multiple things, and we get paralyzed and do not press forward toward whatever it is we desire in our lives. I am convinced that if we removed a lot of these distractions, we would find the time to read and grow ourselves, which ultimately would give us more time to create meaningful things in our lives that produce happiness, joy, and fulfillment. But these things don't happen overnight; it's a process.

I wonder how drastically we would change our behaviors if we saw immediate results. If immediately after eating a doughnut or slice of pizza, we gained five to six pounds, we would quickly stop eating those things. At the same time, that's one of the reasons people don't read, because reading promises to give you change over time, and we live in an instant culture. There's instant coffee, affirmation through social media, and fast food. When reading, or taking the time to read, you develop yourself slowly in the oven. Here's what I know about cooking food in the oven as opposed to the microwave: it stays hot longer, and you enjoy what you cook. When using the microwave, chances are it's a quick, on-the-go type of meal, and the food does not stay hot as long. I'm convinced that if you were to take the journey into reading, over time you would grow to love it, and you would grow as a person. The question is, Will you do it?

Review

1. Do you like reading? Why or why not?
2. Have you ever had a traumatic experience that affected your love of reading?
3. What have you enjoyed reading that has grown you as a person?
4. How can reading impact your life?
5. Do you believe "leaders are readers"? Why or why not?

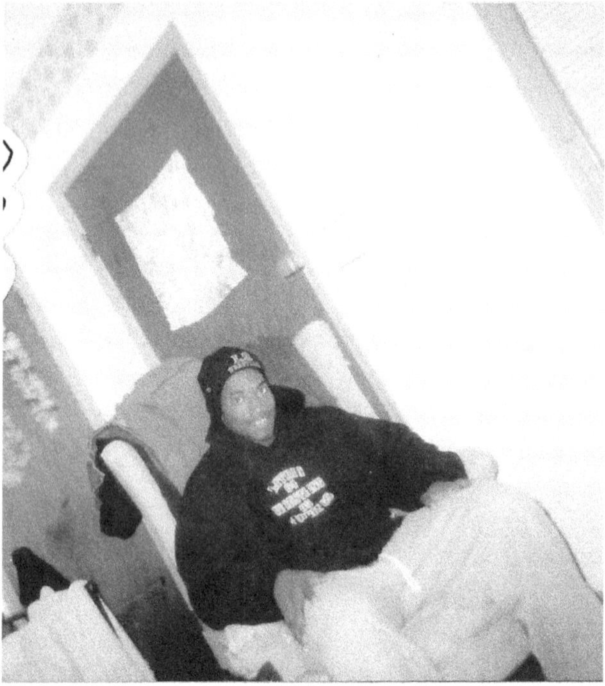

CHAPTER 11

I Wish I Knew That What I Do Today Will Affect My Tomorrow

> Education is the passport to the future, for tomorrow belongs to those who prepare for it today.
> —Malcolm X

Sometimes, we as men see our lives in different compartments. We do not realize that life is a bunch of connected events that happens for us, not to us. The way I take care of today affects my tomorrow. So often, we get caught up in thinking that success is something that will happen for us overnight, and we think that if we do something one time, it should get us to our desired destination. This is not the case at all. Life is a series of connected events, but in order to make a dream become a reality, I must choose today and master it. Ray Lewis said, "Greatness is a bunch of small things done well." Mastering today ultimately sets us up to be great. My goal is for every man to be inspired to step into his full potential, but I know it's going to be a long, difficult rode, one that is going to require a lot of sacrifice, pain, and sleepless nights. I know it will be worth it. I can't predict the future, but I know I can master today. That's something that I wish I knew when I was younger.

I Did Not Know

In middle school, I did not know that my today affects my tomorrow. I thought life was just a bunch of random events that happened to me, not for me. I didn't see how they were interwoven to create an overwhelming, big picture for my life, and in some essence my story. In middle school, I did not grasp the concept that if I do not prepare today, I can't expect future success.

In middle school, I had the privilege of playing in the orchestra. The first instrument I played was the violin. I remember being the only guy in the class, which in middle school wasn't a bad thing; it was actually pretty cool because I was surrounded by the ladies. This was sixth grade, and I was pretty bad at it. It wasn't until seventh and eighth grade that I started to pick up the double bass. Then I became better at my craft. When I would practice in class, playing the instrument, I would get a little better. Now looking back, I see the mistake I made. I never took the violin home to practice. I never mastered the day by practicing a craft that would eventually affect my tomorrow. I didn't see how the two coincided—how practicing and working hard today would affect the outcome of a future event tomorrow. I wish I understood that if I wanted to be great, it would take preparation and practice. I don't know how I thought I was going to be a great violinist or bass player without constant practice.

As men, we must know that the decisions we make today ultimately affect our tomorrow. I saw this played out in middle school. One guy on the football team with us got involved with a girl who was known to be around guys socially. The guy got caught being with her, and it caused a bunch of trouble for him. He was kicked off the football team, and if I'm not mistaken, he had to change schools. Granted, he was in middle school, and he made a simple mistake, but what would've happened if he had thought about the ramifications of his decision to get involved with this young lady? I think that would have affected his actions, which would have affected his future, and I probably wouldn't be writing about that situation right now. Think of something in your life that, if you had chosen to look at it from a future standpoint, you would have done differently. Understanding that today affects tomorrow is something that grows on you over time. That's what happened for me when I entered high school.

I Started to Figure It Out

I started to figure this concept out when I was in high school. One specific way I realized how my today affects my tomorrow was when I got my first car. Let me set the scene. The previous summer, I lived in Lithia Springs, Georgia, with no public transportation. The following year, I was determined to have some mode of transportation because I wanted to get out and drive around and hang out with friends. I'm not saying I didn't get a chance to do that, but I did not have my own car. There's something special about being a teenager and having your own car; it gives you a sense of ownership and makes you feel one step closer to adulthood. Well, I remember seeing this one car parked in the driveway of a house when I used to ride the school bus. Every day, I would look at that car and say to myself, "That's going to be my car." As Christmas approached, my parents asked me what I wanted as a gift, and I said, "A car." They asked me again on another day, and I again said that I wanted a car. Over time, that was just my lingo. I would drop hints. I would take them to the place and show them the car. I would pray about it, and it filled my mind. I was consumed with the idea of having my own car. Christmas rolled around, and I got all the presents, and then I was told to step outside. Guess what was there waiting for me? The car I had been asking for. It was a '93 all-white Ford Probe. Keep in mind I did not know how much the car cost. I don't even think the car was originally for sale, but it worked out in such a way that my parents were able to get the car for me at a very reasonable price. That was one of the moments in my life where I understood that how I prepared for today with my mind-set, my thoughts, my words, my actions, and my beliefs would affect my tomorrow.

Growth Happens from Within

During my college years, I slowly gained the realization that growth happens from within. It is a maturing process that happens over time. During my college years, I started to learn the value of my growth and how it would affect my tomorrow.

In college, I understood the value of studying and was hell-bent on doing well on a future test. It was more for my major classes that I homed in on the skill of studying for tests. It was because I actually wanted to do the things in real life that I prepared to study for mastery. And that grew me as a person. I started to become more confident because I knew that I was putting in the work—the work that no one saw, the work that no one knew about, the work that would ultimately change my tomorrow. That's what I figured out in college. I learned that my today will ultimately affect my tomorrow. The new skills that I learned inside the classroom setting, the relationships that I formed with other classmates, these would ultimately affect my tomorrow.

Our tomorrows demand a new version of ourselves that we have yet to see. The only thing you and I can do today to prepare for tomorrow is to embrace our own evolution.

I Tried to Own My Today

It's so empowering to understand that I, Keith Collins, can own my day, which will ultimately affect my tomorrow. This belief can be applied to many of my relationships. How I interact today with my son will affect our relationship tomorrow. At one time, I had one son, and I wanted so badly for him to understand how much I loved him, so daily I would tell him, hug him, kiss him, and just communicate to him how much I love him. I didn't always get it right, and there were days where my frustration and nagging as a parent limited me in communicating how much I loved him. I let it get in the way of the future relationship that I wanted with him. Over time, he has grown, and now he is an older brother. I still master today by showing him love and affection that I have toward him. And one of the coolest things is now I get an opportunity to watch him display the same love to his younger brother. We have this thing we do. Before Jeremiah goes off to school, he gives his mother and his brother a kiss on the nose. That's his way of communicating "I love you" to them before he leaves. I believe that happens because I made the choice years ago to master every day with my son.

You might say to yourself, "Man, I've messed up. There's no possible way I can repair a relationship that will produce results like that." I'm not asking you to be me. I'm asking you to take responsibility for your today. The results take care of themselves. Your job is to do your part and master today. A farmer's job is to plant a seed and water it. He's not in control of the rain, the sunlight, or anything that might happen to that seed in the midst of him sleeping. His job is to focus on controlling what he can control, and that's the whole premise of this chapter—to control what you can control. As I mentioned earlier, the only thing you can control is your attitude and your actions. Case closed. That's it. So that means, so what if someone wronged you, so what if they hurt your feelings, so what if they have taken advantage of you. That was yesterday; I am talking about today. What choices will you make to better your future and your family's future? It starts today with your preparation for the goal you want tomorrow.

The Value of Preparation

Have you ever baked a cake? Baking a cake requires a lot of preparation on the front end, before you get a chance to taste that warm, delicate, sweet, chocolatey, sensational cake. There's much preparation that goes into making something that tastes so good. There's the preparation of getting the eggs, the flour, the sugar, the butter, the vanilla extract, the chocolate chips, the cocoa powder, and of course the pan to put the batter in. Preparation takes us on a journey.

Preparation is designed to build up our character, so when we face opposition, we confidently know how to react and respond. I think of the football player who practices catching the ball in the end zone and puts both his feet down just in time, before the defender pushes him out of bounds. He practices that move days on end in hopes that when game time comes, his body will automatically react as if it was at practice, because he's gone through that motion numerous times. How often have you practiced a desired goal, visualizing it inside your head, seeing it inside your mind, going through the motions mentally and physically in preparation for that big day? Or are you one of those people who show up and rely on your talent? I heard it said that your talent gets you in the room, and your character keeps you in the room. Your character refers to your preparation, who you are when no one is watching. That's what keeps you in the room, and that's why preparation is so valuable. It's when no one is watching. Because here's one thing I know: who you are in the dark will always come to light. I've always wanted to like what I see in the light, so I must make a conscious decision every day, in the dark places of my life and in the times when no one is watching, to do the most I can to prepare for the day. As I'm writing this book, I'm sitting in my car early in the morning around four o'clock, when no one is around. That's what preparation looks like.

Thinking toward the Future

What is the goal or dream that you have in your heart that maybe no one knows about? If you do not have one, I encourage you and challenge you to pray and ask God for one. Here's why: when you think about your future, it pulls at you, it tugs at you, and it stretches you. When we think about our future and where we would like to be, it causes us to ask the question, How do I get there? That's a powerful question because that question then gives you answers, and those answers challenge you to do something. I want you to think about your future. I want you to see yourself being the father, husband, business owner, and role model you want to be. But of course, those things do not happen if we're not thinking. So often we get caught up in survival mode, to where we only want to survive for today. Here's a newsflash: if you're preparing for today right now, it's a little too late. The you that you are today is a result of your thoughts and habits of yesterday. So if you want to change the outcome of who you are going to be tomorrow, you must change who you are today. You must take on a new persona today. Time waits for no one, so there's no saying, "Oh, I will do it tomorrow." You and I have only today. Tomorrow is the future that we will not see, because when we see it, it will then be the present—just like today.

How to Make Decisions

Here's a quick little formula that I picked up years ago from a pastor friend of mine, Andy Stanley. He was talking to the congregation and giving them a sure way to make better decisions and live without regrets. It's something that I decided to put in this book because I know the value of his role in my life. Here are the simple steps that you and I can take today to better our tomorrow. It's composed of three questions all rolled into one. In spite of my past experiences, in spite of my current situation, in spite of my future hopes and dreams, what is the wise thing to do? That's it. This simple question will help us make better decisions and live without regrets, which will ultimately help us to win today to affect our tomorrow. I really hope that you and I can grasp this concept, to openly redirect and change the trajectory of decisions we have made or will make, so we can impact our future and the future lives of those we live with. Ultimately, by making better decisions and caring about our today, we model for others how to take ownership of the day, as opposed to allowing the day to happen to us. It is my prayer that you live out today with purpose, just like the apostle Paul wrote in Ephesians 5:15 (NIV). It says to be careful how you live, not as unwise but wise.

Review

1. What are your current beliefs about owning today?
2. Has your life modeled that belief up until this point?
3. In what ways can the wisdom from this chapter help you in your current life situation?

4. Name a time when you did not make a wise choice. How did it affect you?
5. What action steps can you take today to live a better tomorrow?

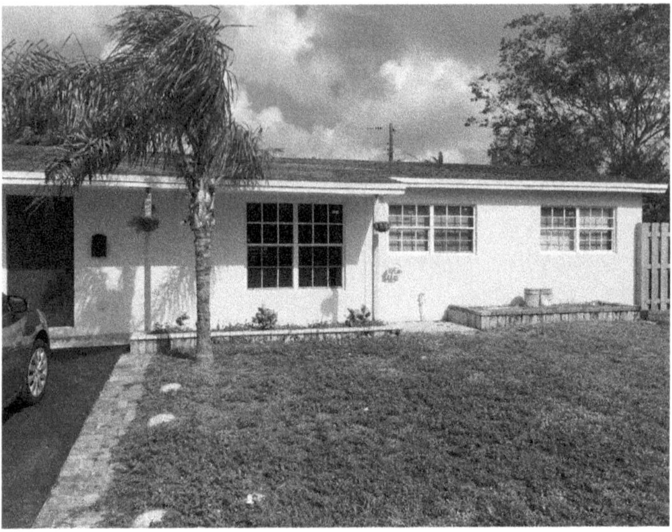

CHAPTER 12

I Wish I Knew That Managing My Finances Was So Important

*If you will live like no one else, later
you can live like no one else.*
— Dave Ramsey

Money, money, money, money. It's funny how this one word can change the course of relationships and is the topic of a lot of conversations. Many people fail to realize how taking ownership of it can drastically change the trajectory of relationships, businesses, confidence, and families' futures. I've heard it said that money is the root of all evil. That's a lie; the Bible says in 1 Timothy 6:10 (NIV) that the love of money is the root of all evil. This love for money, which a lot of people have, comes from our lack of understanding. Money is a tool, and like any tool, it's neither good or bad; it just depends on the user. It's important for us to learn how to use what we have been blessed with. We need to learn how to manage it. To be honest with you, management is not the best word. It is more like proper stewardship, because when you steward something, you understand that it is a gift. And that's something that I wish I knew as a boy.

When I was in middle school, my family was not rich. We lived in apartments and other areas like the projects. We saw other families struggle like we did. The crazy thing is when you are involved in financial struggles and everyone else around you is involved in financial struggles, you don't necessarily understand that that's not the reality of everyone's life. In middle school, I did not understand that there were others out there who were successful and who did not have financial struggles in their homes.

As a kid, I did not understand the value of money because every chance I had to get some money, I spent it all. I remember finding a quarter in the house and going up to our neighborhood corner store to purchase a Little Debbie Strawberry Shortcake Roll, and occasionally I would get the Zebra Cakes. These items brought so much joy to my little face. I remember scouring the house to look for the quarters, and when I would find them … man, was I happy. As soon as the money came into my hand, I went to the store. I spent it with no remorse or understanding. I remember having to ask my dad for money when I was younger, because he did not live with me at the time, and occasionally I needed money for school clothes. This became so common between me and my dad that I was able to finish his statement before he even said, "I do not have it." I did not understand how speaking those words, "I do not have," only continue to perpetuate the lack. As I grew up, I thought I would have. That desire transformed into a job when I got to high school.

I Worked a Little

Through parts of middle school and throughout high school, I occasionally worked with my stepfather. He owned a painting company. That was where I learned the value of hard work and an appreciation for money when it came into my hands. He often joked with me, saying, "You want everything in the world, until it comes down to spending your own money." But isn't that the role of a teenager, to want to get the latest shoes? On a consistent basis, I tried to avoid having to spend my own money.

My thoughts were to make the money and keep it all to myself. I did not understand the concept of being generous and giving to others. I did not think of the money as a gift from God to me, and it definitely was not something I could see myself giving away to a church. The only things I would spend my money on were the pleasures of life—some clothes for when I went back to school and some shoes. It wasn't until I was spending the money for these things that I understood how much they cost. Have you ever had to make a decision between a fresh pair Nikes and some knockoff shoes because you wanted an extra twenty dollars in your pocket? You didn't want to spend fifty? Eventually, I would get better at understanding how to manage the money I was given.

In College, I Tried to Stay Away from Debt

In college, I tried to stay away from debt. Upon entering college, I only knew one thing—that I did not want to have to pay for it. To be honest with you, I am a cheap guy at heart. I don't like spending too much money on anything. So when I began college, I wanted to make sure I was able to have it completely paid for without having to put that financial burden on my family. Because, if you remember earlier in this chapter, where I grew up, everyone struggled, and you don't really understand the struggle until you look back. So when I left high school, my main focus was to get into a college that was not too expensive and that, if necessary, I could afford to pay for on my own. After prayer and much searching, I was able to find an institution that accepted me, and I was able to receive government funding for college.

It was in college where I was able to work and save up some money and buy cars, new speakers, and tons of other things. Again, I fell into the trap of spending the money I had as soon as I got the money. One of the craziest things I used to spend money on was Atlanta fitted hats. I had a collection of more than thirty hats. I would get a paycheck and go spend some money on a hat. One thing I did start to do when I was in college was give to the local church. This was a concept I had learned, and I thought it made sense.

A tithe is basically giving to God 10 percent of any money you make. You might ask yourself, "Why in the world would I give back to God one-tenth of anything I make?" I started to understand God a little bit more, including all he had done for me. Up until that point, I had not spent any money on my schooling, I had a vehicle that I did not have a car payment on, and I had a steady job where I had received multiple promotions. The tithe was a way to consistently say, "Thank you, God!" I used to get confused and think that God needed money. In actuality, anything that I give back to Him, He had already given it to me in the first place. So with that understanding, I learned that I was a steward. A person who stewards something knows that what they have is not theirs in the first place; it's kind of like being a renter. When you rent a home, you know the home is not yours. Your job is to live in it and to maintain it while you're there. That's what I was thinking about in terms of my finances. So one thing I started to do while I was in college was be faithful with my tithe. It radically changed my financial outlook. In Malachi 3:10 (NIV), it talks about God asking people to give to the local church. By doing so, God continues to bless you by your obedience and your faithfulness to His house. In Matthew 6:33 (NIV), it talks about seeking God first, and all the other things will be added onto you—and this is one way of my seeking God first, in the area of my finances. In college, I stayed blessed. I went through two automobiles that were totaled because of car wrecks, and I was always able to have transportation. That's just one example of how I believe staying faithful with the tithe and learning how to manage my finances affected me. I would eventually make some mistakes in the area of my finances and would have to learn some hard lessons.

Now at the age of thirty, I can look back over the last years of my life. I got into and out of debt, and it was not easy, but it was doable. Well, that might be a little straightforward. First, I got married. In the Bible, it speaks about two people becoming one, and that was like the marriage found in Genesis 2:24 (NIV) between Adam and Eve. It says, "For this reason, a man shall leave his father and mother and cleave to his wife," meaning the joining of the union. If I'm going to believe the Bible, I'm going to believe the whole thing. So my wife and I joined our finances together. We wanted to live the American dream, so we went and bought a car. That added to our debt, and then when we got a house, and we needed to pay for stuff in the house because we didn't want to live in an empty house. So we got a couple of credit cards and purchased items to fill the house and not put a spotlight on the fact that we didn't have money. We bought a lot of furniture. Then we noticed how convenient it was to have a credit card to supplement for the lack of income—or the lack of knowledge of how to manage our finances. So we used the credit card whenever our paychecks did not finish paying for meals. That snowballed, and within three years, our credit card debt amounted to about $30,000. That was when we decided to do something about it.

Keep in mind we tried to do something about it a couple times before, but it quickly got out of the scope of our knowledge and expertise. So we looked for other resources to help us manage our finances most effectively. That's when we took a strong look at Dave Ramsey's Financial Peace University course. This is a course on how to handle finances, and I highly recommend it. That led to us taking our finances seriously. We established a budget, prayed, and asked God to help us with the organization of our debt. Then we took the steps in the financial peace course as they told us to. It's funny, because the same time we started taking the course seriously is when we received all the changes in our lot. We started a budget and maintained it, and God did the rest. In a year and a half, we paid off that $30,000 debt. John Maxwell said a budget is telling your money where to go; you don't wonder where it went.

I am thoroughly convinced that as you take care of your finances, you will find yourself being able to do more and become more than you ever thought possible. In Matthew 6:21 (NIV) and Luke 12:24 (NIV), it talks about where your treasure is, your heart will also be. And a lot of times, our treasure is not in the things that we say are most important to us—and that's because we find ourselves accumulating money that already has an obligation before we are given an opportunity to do great in the world. I think that says something about us as men—when we're able to look at ourselves and be honest with ourselves and say, "Hey, we can improve in this area." I hope to convey to you through my story that it is possible to be debt-free and take care of your finances, which will ultimately put you closer to your dreams and goals.

Delayed Gratification

If we're honest with ourselves, no one wants to be broke and struggling. So what keeps us broke and in the struggle? I believe it's our inability to practice the habit of delayed gratification. Now, if I'm going to say delayed gratification is a problem in our society, I must explain what delayed gratification is. Delayed gratification is the ability to put off something immediate for a larger and greater future something. It's the discipline not to buy that item that you know you can't afford to save for something that's going to be a much greater reward. When we're able to master delaying immediate satisfaction for future enjoyment, that's when we are able to grab hold of our finances. But why is it so hard?

We live in an instant and highly celebrated culture. We see someone with something that we don't have, and we believe that we are supposed to have it too—and at the same time, probably even faster. This type of mentality is deadly. I believe we all have a specific dream and calling and a pathway in life. Each of us has a specific timing for things to happen and manifest. There are appropriate steps that allow us to enjoy the success we have in a more fulfilling light. I've heard it said that anything that is gained without hard work is seldom truly appreciated. This practice of self-discipline teaches us to appreciate the process. The process is hardly ever celebrated; we celebrate the product. In football, we only recognize how hard some of our top quarterback athletes work to perfect their craft. On game day, when they score the touchdown, we think they're in the perfect position to be successful. We often don't realize how much practice or how many hours went into perfecting the craft. We see the highlight reels of other people's lives through social media platforms like Instagram and Twitter and Facebook, but we don't see the day-to-day realness and sacrifices that need to be made. If we set financial goals and are willing to sacrifice to achieve those goals, we will soon experience the success on the other side, and then we will enjoy the success, knowing that we gained it the right way, and we will know that if we were to lose it all, we could easily gain it back.

So, how do you make delayed gratification a part of your everyday life? I believe it trickles from the little things. Being willing to not buy something that you want with your credit card, saving up for it instead. Set a goal, write down the goal, keep the goal in front of you everywhere you go, and act on the goal by making the process part of the fulfillment of achieving the goal. Whenever you find yourself with the opportunity to get immediate gratification, put it off to a later date. Put it off for another moment in time. Sometimes I get caught up in finding stuff on the internet that I want to buy. And usually I want to go ahead and grab it that same day because I get all hyped up and energized for it, so what I do is wait a day or two. In that time, my want for the item will grow or dissipate. I might find something else to take its place. That's one way that I practice delayed gratification.

Budgets Work

Often, when we hear the word "budget," we get frightened. We think of what we can't get. In reality, budgets help you get exactly what you want. Budgets are like road maps to your financial dreams. Budgets help you to see what's doable in certain seasons of life. To be honest with you, I'm no expert when it comes to budgeting. My wife handles a lot of the budgets. But she and I have a clear understanding of our goals and necessities and the things we want to accomplish, so that makes it easy for us to say no to certain things in certain seasons. A budgets allows you to do just that. It teaches you how to say no to things that are not aligned with the overall goal. I recommend taking Dave Ramsey's Financial Peace course to gain more knowledge and insight on how to budget effectively.

Review

1. What is your household belief about finances?
2. How have those beliefs affected you?
3. What are your thoughts on accumulating debt?
4. What steps are you currently taking to master your finances and generate wealth for your family?
5. What are some of your long-term financial goals?

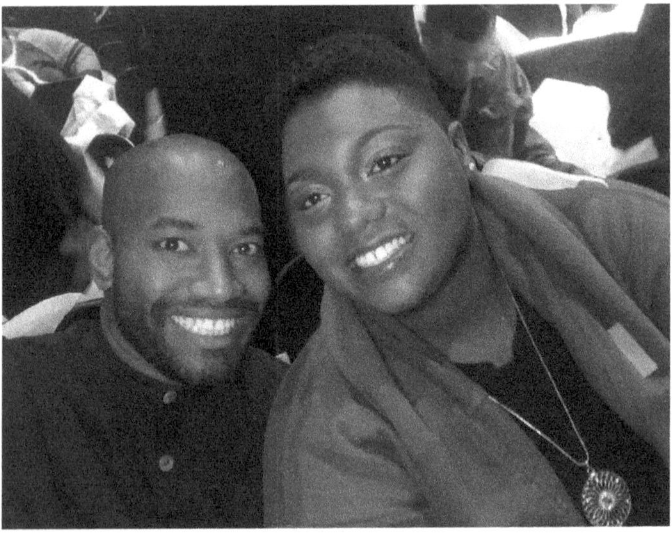

CHAPTER 13

I Wish I Knew That Taking Care of My Mental Health Mattered

Don't fake being okay. You only hurt yourself. Be real with what you're going through. Just don't let it consume you.
—Unknown

Suppose you were to have a car for the rest of your life and could never trade it in. How would you take care of it? I know I would always be watching the car, keeping it clean, making sure I stayed up to date on the maintenance of the car. I would make sure that no harm came to it. I would put the right type of gasoline in it and make sure it always had the right oil levels. I would cherish the car because it was the only one I would ever have. Well, our bodies are just like that. They are complex and hard-driven machines. And it's our job as individuals—as men—to take care of it. It's funny how we often don't see our bodies as a temple that's going to allow us to achieve all that God has for us. This is something that I wish I knew as a boy—that how I take care of this body over the course of my life will determine my future hopes and dreams.

I Was Doing It without Knowing It

I was doing it without knowing it, not taking care of my body. As a kid, I loved to eat sweets—and I still do. I ate cakes, pies, chips, and Kool-Aid. It was around the house. My pop called me the human garbage disposal. I would eat and eat and eat and eat—and play tons of video games as well. I found myself eating and playing games, and next thing I knew, a whole entire day had gone by. Slowly but surely, I gained weight. I remember going to the mall and shopping at J. C. Penney and having to get husky-size clothing. I called myself pleasantly plump, and I had man boobs. But I was in middle school and I did not have to take my weight super seriously. At least I didn't think I did. I was 170 pounds. Now, that gets you in only one sport—football—and I was the center for my middle school football team.

As a kid, I didn't understand how my diet or exercising would affect me in the long term. The only thing I could understand is that sweets were good, veggies lacked taste, and exercise happened only if I played basketball. There were a couple of moments in my middle school career that I realized that I wasn't in the best shape possible. It was when I had to chase friends who were smaller than me in a game of tag. I did manage to make the track team in middle school. It was not because of my speed; it was because of my ability to throw the shot put. As I left middle school, I started to understand the importance of weight training and overall conditioning.

I Worked Out a Little Bit More

Upon entering high school, I quickly learned that my natural abilities would not get me far in the field of athletics if I did not train. So I began to work out with the football team and take weight training as a class. If I'm going to be honest with you: it was intimidating. There were guys in the weight room who could lift hundreds of pounds more than I could. There were guys in the weight room who had high school records. Talk about feeling inferior. Overall, I understood that if I wanted to be better than I currently was, I would have to start somewhere. And that's what I learned, that I had to start somewhere, and I had to start with actually exercising more. I did that for the first two years of high school. And then I realized that I knew nothing until my junior and senior years.

As I mentioned earlier, I started wrestling in my junior year. And for any of you guys who have ever wrestled, you know that that's how you get in shape. Wrestling is a full-fledged HIIT workout—high-intensity interval training. That's all wrestling is, and it felt like we did it all day long. I remember sprawling with some of my teammates. I remember sacrificing eating food or junk food on Thanksgiving so I could be in shape for tournaments. I remember having to run miles; to this day, I do not know how many miles I ran. In high school, at my lowest weight, I was 156 pounds, and I wrestled the 160 weight class. Talk about transformation. My body was ripped. I felt strong, quick, and light on my feet, and I was excited to be able to run and catch up with those people who were right in front of me. I guess you can say I found myself liking that man in the mirror. I was a sexy beast, if I do say so myself. But the good looks and nice body quickly faded upon graduation.

I Let Myself Go

Upon graduating high school, I went to college and worked full-time. I started to eat unhealthily. Fries were a staple in my diet. I ate them every single day. The soft drinks and all of the sugar I was consuming started to catch up with me, and I blossomed into a nice 210 pounds. Now that I look back, I can see the growth in my waistline. I went up to close to a thirty-eight waistline.

During this time in college, I took courses about health, but I didn't focus on or appreciate what the teacher was trying to tell me. I fell into the trap of thinking that I was young and invincible, and because of that, I did not need to exercise on a consistent basis. If I had money, I could buy clothes, and if I can buy clothes, I'm good. But I watched the size of my clothes increase, which led to the normal comparisons with other guys my age who looked slimmer. The further I got into adulthood, the more I realizes the importance of proper health.

When I say proper health, I'm not talking about running marathons, eating kale salads for breakfast, lunch, and dinner, and drinking water all the time. I'm talking about a healthy understanding of food and the role it plays in our lives, and how it can make us tired or make us energized. I started to eat food for energy. And what I know about energy is you use it and you store it, so that's what I started to do. I only ate food as a source of energy. I ate because I knew I had to.

Now at the age of thirty, I understand why my health is important. I get that cardiovascular disease is the number one cause of death among males. Most of the diseases are found in the gut area of men. I want to be around for my kids. When I turned thirty, I started to be a little bit more disciplined with how late I ate, how often I exercised, and the food I ate.

I would love to live a long and healthy life. I want to be there to watch my kids grow up and accomplish their dreams and impact others. I want to be an active parent in my children's lives, so that means I must take care of myself, and that's one of the reasons that I figured out health was important.

By all means, I am no health expert, but I have picked up a couple things that work for me, which has allowed me to avoid gaining so much additional weight. I have learned to watch out for highly processed foods. This means, as much as possible, I limit my intake of foods that I could not find in natural environments. When foods go through a huge processing process, it takes away a lot of the essential nutrients and vitamins that are needed to maintain a good base level of health. This is also one of the reasons why our genes mutate (i.e., how cancer shows up). I'm not saying you have to be a processed-food police; I'm just saying watch what you eat. You are what you eat, just like people become what they think about.

How to Stay Healthy

Upon turning thirty, I had to learn how to work out, and to be honest with you, I don't enjoy it. I hate having to think about what to do, when to move, how much to move, and how often to move, so I dedicate thirty minutes a day to doing movement. With this simple process, I've seen great results, which has allowed me to maintain my weight and not see such huge fluctuations.

I have to watch what I eat, and that means reading labels. You would be surprised what goes into our normal foods because of the mass production and preservation process. By doing research and finding out what goes into your foods, you make yourself aware, and one thing I know about being aware is that it requires you to either confront or neglect, to move on whatever information you have learned.

Being a guy, it's important to have your yearly physical and annual checkups because what you don't know can hurt you. I want to stick around for a lot of reasons—for my kids and my kids' kids' kids. So I must be willing to find out the information to be healthy. My father-in-law and my stepfather both were able to beat major health crisis because of annual visits to the doctor. We as men cannot allow the fear of going to the doctor to cripple us from finding out things that we need to know, things we can actually do something about. The majority of all diseases are preventable—not curable but preventable.

Manage your stress level. In the Bible, it tells us multiple times to not worry, and I think it's because God is trying to communicate to us that He is in control and we are not. So, as men, have to make sure we manage our stress levels, because if we don't, there are many health risks associated with high levels of stress, including heart attack, strokes, and other complications. One sure way we can manage our stress levels is by having the ability to communicate effectively to our spouses, our children, and our coworkers whenever we feel upset about something. That doesn't mean going off on people and telling them to "catch me outside." But it does mean being able to express and communicate your feelings in a productive manner without having to bottle them up on the inside, where they come out in bits and bouts of rage, which can be devastating for you and the people involved. You are not a four-year-old who throws temper tantrums; you are a man, and a man knows how to communicate. So take these words I have shared with you and apply them and you will see amazing results.

Review

1. What are your views on health? When did those views formulate?
2. What are you doing today to improve your health?
3. How are you managing your stress levels?
4. What is stressing you? Why?
5. What is your diet like? Why is it like that?

FINAL WORDS OF ENCOURAGEMENT

I hope this book has helped you gain a new perspective on your journey to manhood. Know that there might be bumps in the road along the way, but you have been given the tools needed to make this journey to manhood a success. Remember it's not just having knowledge that is power; it's applied knowledge that brings the power. Now it's time for you to go and be the dad, son, and man you've always wanted to be. You have no excuse for not reaching any dream or goal that you set before you. You've got this!

BIBLIOGRAPHY

http://www.drphil.com/advice/the-role-of-the-man-in-the-family/.

https://www.npr.org/sections/ed/2017/06/18/533062607/poverty-dropouts-pregnancy-suicide-what-the-numbers-say-about-fatherless-kids.

https://verilymag.com/2014/11/myths-about-low-self-esteem-debunked.

https://www.telegraph.co.uk/men/thinking-man/scary-effects-pornography-21st-centurys-accute-addiction-rewiring/.

https://knowhownonprofit.org/people/people-management-skills/change/basics-on-managing-change/fivesteps.

ABOUT THE AUTHOR

Keith Collins grew up in southwest Atlanta, where he faced many different challenges and obstacles. For a great part of his childhood, he was raised by a single mom. After graduating high school, he attended the University of West Georgia, where he earned a bachelor's degree in marketing and management. After graduation, he relocated to South Florida, where he married his wife, Stania.

Keith Collins has been working in the nonprofit market for more than five years, and for the last three years, he has been speaking to thousands. As a speaker, his passion is to encourage youth and adults to step out of their comfort zone and push past their self-imposed limitations. He specializes in helping men who have been affected by broken promises and missed opportunities. He helps transformation happen. He works with men of all ages who are facing life challenges and are looking to create change.

His clients are servant-leaders who are looking to help their students, leaders, and organizations push past self-imposed limitations. He desires to partner with you to transform lives and men around the country.

Booking info: www.keithcollins360.com

Lightning Source UK Ltd.
Milton Keynes UK
UKHW041843280219
338226UK00001B/20/P